WILEY-ACADEMY

JAN KAPLICKY

CONFESSIONS

TO MY ONLY FRIEND, JOSEF KAPLICKY JNR.

CONTENT

CONFESSIONS — 8

PRINCIPLES — 13

FREEDOM / CREATIVITY / VISION / PLASTICITY / BEAUTY / POETRY / ELEGANCE / SENSUALITY / SEXUALITY / PEOPLE / COLOUR

ARCHITECTURE — 49

NEW PROFESSION / EUROPE / SOCIAL FACTOR / CULTURE / POLITICS / FROM ABOVE / DISTANCE / EVOLUTION / KITSCH / ECO / GREEN SPACE / STRUCTURE / MATERIAL / PLANT / DETAIL

PROCESS — 87

PROCESS / INFLUENCES / DIALOGUE / ANONYMOUS CREATORS / CONFUSION / FOOD + DRINK / TOOLS / BRAIN + MACHINE / RESEARCH + TESTING / 1000 + 1 PEOPLE / DIARY / SKETCH / DRAWING / PHOTOMONTAGE / MODEL + MOCK-UP / DESIGN / ARCHITECTURE

LIFE — 131

LIFE / IN MY LIFETIME / JOSEF KAPLICKY / JIRINA KAPLICKA / 1937 - 2001 / TODAY / FUTURE / LAST WORD

BIOGRAPHY — 204

'ONE CAN DRIVE

A MAGNIFICENT CADILLAC OR JAGUAR

OR ONE CAN BE PASSIONATELY DEVOTED TO

ONES WORK.'

LE CORBUSIER, 1965

1.

2.

WRITTEN IN...

3.

4.

5.

1. Cote d'Azur, France.
2. Prague, Czech Republic
3. London, England.
4. Provence, France.
5. Martha's Vineyard, United States.
6. Umbria, Italy.
7. Oliveto, Italy.

6.

7.

7

CONFESSIONS

What is here to confess? All? Something? Nothing? It is all about what you feel inside, as architect, as individual, as man? How to express your feelings within your work? How to resist so many wrong temptations? Commercial pressures. Financial needs. Comforts. Glory. Poverty. Survival. Attacks. Jealousy. Arrogance. Very rarely praises. How to survive horrible people, bad television, bad books, ugly people? How to be strong enough every single morning, organise your mind, and above all create something? I have endless admiration for those who accomplish this, particularly for those who went to war, prison, were ill, were prosecuted, and still managed to achieve an enormous amount. Those who never lost their professional and human integrity and dignity.

**'Someday I would like to write a book about everything and the people I met.'
JK, 7/9/70**

1. Le Corbusier's grave. 2. Love. 3. V. Havel. 4. 'Voyager' aeroplane. 5. Human brain. 6. Dancer and Parthenon. 7. J. Glenn, astronaut. 8. Lovers.

1.
2.
3.
4.
5.
6.
7.
8.

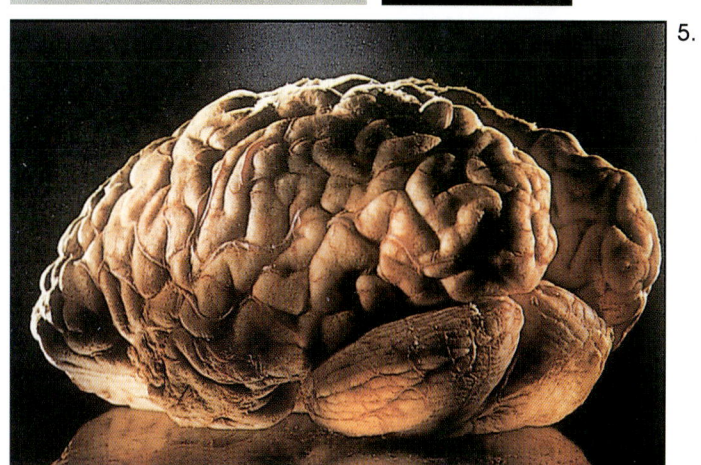

9

CONFESSIONS

There are people who are liberated enough to express their true feelings to themselves. People who can say their true feelings to others. That requires enormous will and strength. There are still too many good people destroyed by others. Too many people who know very little are being glorified. This is true at any time in life. Life requires knowledge, skill, patience, and above all sensitivity. How to carry on, how to create without useless meetings? Useless people. Useless statements. How to live mentally and physically? What will happen to your child? What is right and what is wrong? How to enjoy life? How to be creative? How to relax? How to design? What to design? How not to be destructive? When to smile? When to almost cry? These apply above all in architecture, which is my life, and not just my profession.

1. E. Hemingway. 2. Le Corbusier, Une Petite Maison. 3. O. Niemeyer. 4. Buildings, 2001. 5. Beach. 6. Rock Island. 7. Soviet prison. 8. A. Solzhenitsyn in Gulag.

1.
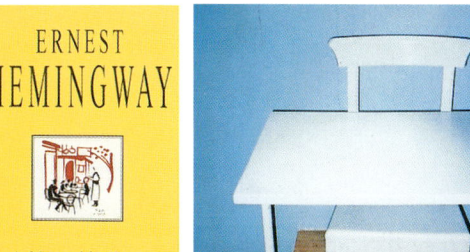

2.

3.

4.

5.

6.

7.

8.
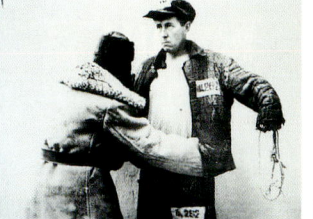

11

PRINCIPLES

FREEDOM

Freedom of speech. Freedom of expression. Freedom of form. Freedom of decision. Freedom of information. All this was denied me for many years. Altogether for 26 years. Almost half of my life. This is why I will always treasure these freedoms. The fascists or communists tried to destroy everything. The Iron Curtain went down – no books, no passports, jamming of radio, more prisons, no education, no to just everything. Something new was banned everyday. When I now see groups of students travelling freely through Europe I envy them. I almost cry. I hope they treasure every moment. When I see people not interested in books, magazines, information, I despair. For me it was a desperate battle to see and know more. I despair when I see young architects not even bother to open a book or magazine – a privilege I never had. I had to learn everything myself. Architecture can never prosper in dictatorship of any form. Freedom of expression must be at the beginning of any design process. You can build only in a democracy. You can create only in freedom.

'Democracy builds.' F. L. Wright

1. A. Solzhenitsyn. 2. Berlin 1989. 3. Prague 1989. 4. Liberty stamp. 5. Balkan War, 1995. 6. Iron Curtain. 7. New York, 11/09/2001. 8. Prague 1989. 9. Berlin 1989.

1.

ALEXANDER
SOLZHENITSYN
THE GULAG
ARCHIPELAGO

2.

3.

4.

U.S. POSTAGE 3¢
IN GOD WE TRUST
LIBERTY

5.

6.

7.

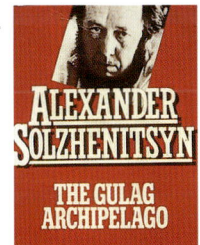

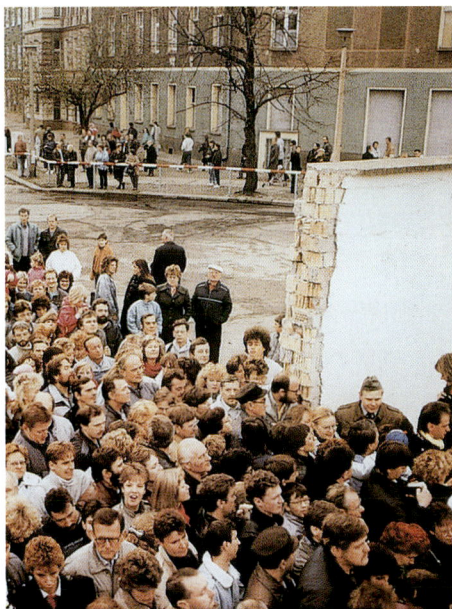

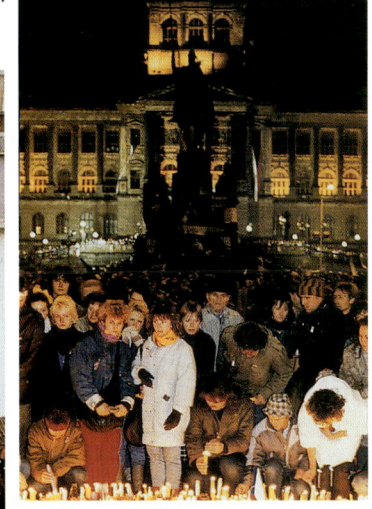

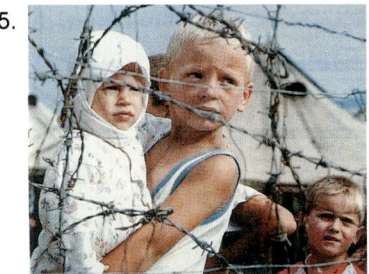

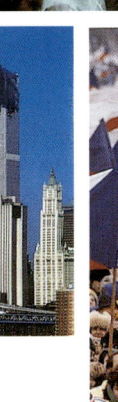

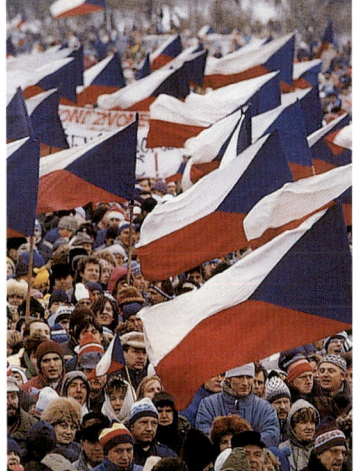

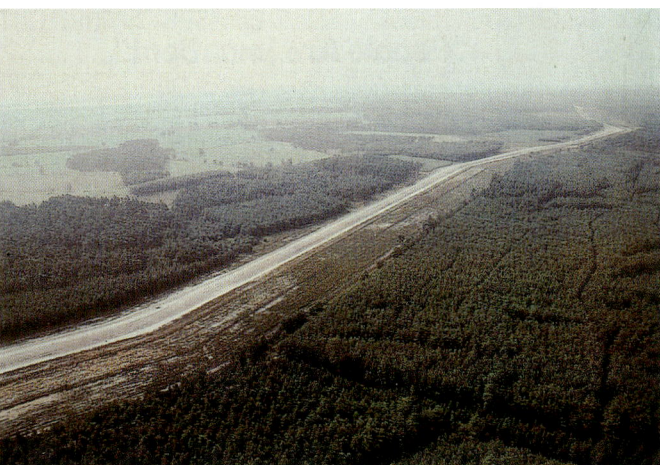

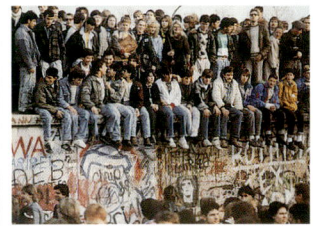

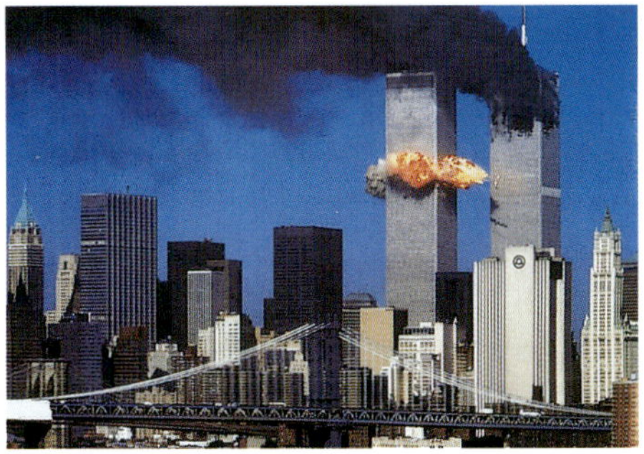

8.

9.

CREATIVITY

Creativity certainly does exist, though it might be denied by a few. You can see the results everywhere. Some still try to say creativity does not exist. Just because they are not creative themselves. It could be a simple structure by a three-year-old child, to the most sophisticated building, bridge, aeroplane, musical composition, medical solution or computer disk. Creativity has always been here. The only profession that struggles to create is architecture. Again, some deny it. Some say architecture does not need creativity. What a primitive and simplistic statement. On the contrary, I do not see enough of it. I feel that the creative process is a natural and imperative part of the design process of any building, large or small. Safety pin, aluminium sheet, champagne cork, sardine box, Parthenon; all these achieved something. Sometimes thousands of years ago. Sometimes something complex and outstanding. Creativity has been around for thousands of years. It is around now. Nobody can ever deny it.

'Magic architecture is an expression of creativeness.' F. Kiesler

1. Champagne cork. 2. Sea chart. 3. Chinese garden. 4. Paestum Temple. 5. Water drum. 6. Computer disk. 7. Cyclist and bike. 8. Car, 1901.

1.

2.
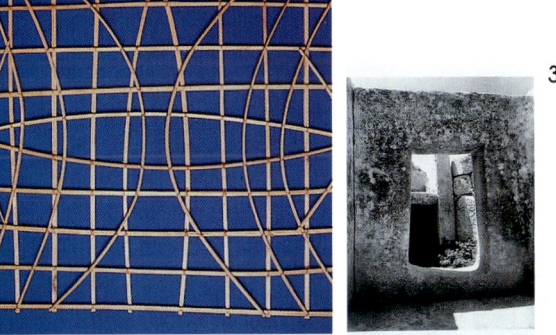

3.

4.

6.

7.

8.

9.

17

CREATIVITY

Let's create something so poetic, colourful and overwhelming as a blue sky. Nobody will dislike it. Let's create beautiful buildings, places, gardens, towns. Let's create things of outstanding beauty, things of simplicity, flexibility and colour. Things of importance, impact and timelessness, cannot be denied. Impact cannot be disputed. Creativity is a lonely process. One or two people, then a whole team, then hundreds involved, supported by many, slowly creating complex objects of today. We are all creators. People who will not be surprised with results. People with strong feelings about the future. People with knowledge. People with strong will. But we are attacked by many hundreds of non-creative people – those who prefer just to sit and talk. It gives me shivers sometimes to see the creative results of past generations, from critical to revolutionary creations. I want to be part of this process. To be creative is one of the biggest challenges and pleasures in the world. Without creativity there is nothing. Nothing at all.

'To create, one must first question everything.' E. Grey

1. Contraceptive pill. 2. Sardine tin, 1824. 3. First wrist watch. 4. A. Kapoor. 5. PAGST helmet, 1986, 6. B-2 bomber. 7. Hip joint. 8. Sahara turban. 9. Sinclair C5 electric car, 1984.

1.

2.

3.

4.

5.

6.

7.

8.

9.

19

VISION

It is not such a long time ago that we could see only the surface of things around us. We had to memorise. Then came photography. Suddenly there was a record available, though only a black-and-white record. Then came colour. Then x-ray photography. We could see inside things, how they are constructed, how they operate, how they function. Reality came closer to us. We can now see much deeper. We can see forms we never thought of. Soon we will have all this in 3-D. We may even be able to smell it. I am sure many architects do not see this amazing development. They are not interested. They are totally immune to new horizons. They mostly ignore these changes. Extraordinary new forms are emerging. Completely new structures. How can we use all this to our advantage, for a truly new world? Some architects will do so, but unfortunately very few. I certainly will.

'Eyes that cannot see.' Le Corbusier

1. Body, 1856. 2. Human head. 3. Eye. 4. Hand. 5. Body, 2002. 6. Breast. 7. Sperm. 8. Embryo.

21

VISION

Our vision possibilities are developing very fast indeed. Not long ago we could see a picture of a pyramid only in black-and-white. We can now see our planet as a globe. This was only 30 years ago. We can see newspapers headlines from 500km above. We can see the coming of hurricanes and monsoons. We can see other planets in detail. This was almost unthinkable a few years ago. We can see stars and planets we did not know about. We can see moon dust or Mars dust. These new dimensions will change global vision, global architecture and urbanism. This is the fourth dimension Le Corbusier was talking about. Colour is another new dimension. Now almost every piece of printing is in colour. Black-and-white print is fashion not necessity. Books, magazines and even newspapers are in colour. We see the world in colour on TV every night. Every event, however horrible, is in colour. A different world. Some architects never open books or magazines. Let's see all these developments as architects, designers and urbanists. Let's see this new world as creators, with totally new possibilities, new visions. A new future.

1. White Horse Hill, England. 2. AATSR–2 image. 3. Planet Earth. 4. Black-and-white pyramids, 1859. 5. Colour pyramids, 2001. 6. Satellite view, 500km above. 7. British Isles from 900km. 8. Underwater image.

PLASTICITY

Plasticity is an integral part of nature. It was here from the beginning. Plasticity of sand dunes, earthforms and sea waves has been here for millions of years. Plasticity of animal bodies. Plasticity of the human body. Plasticity in nature has hundreds of reasons – economy, efficiency, materials and structure to name a few. Whole cultures are using sophisticated plastic form for their structures. Then came the discovery of the straight line, invented entirely by man. Classicism is the almost logical step that followed. This preoccupation with the straight line is certainly a design limitation. In England architects are still creating classical buildings. The straitjacket of the straight line is still with us in the third millennium. It is still in the back of our minds and only a very few are using freedom of plasticity. Even fewer understand the economics, structural advantages and beauty of free form. Particularly beauty. Evolution is essential here. Let's have a new look on the sophistication of forms in nature. Let's study other cultures' forms. Let's open new gates.

'Today we enjoy total plastic freedom.' O. Niemeyer

1. J. Arp. 2. Baroque column. 3. Body. 4. Sand dunes. 5. Iranian house. 6. Greek theatre. 7. Hills, China. 8. Yurta tent.

PLASTICITY

Some architects, engineers, designers, have used free form for generations, some with extraordinary skills and results. There is a whole movement here. Gothic, baroque and more. Since the beginning of the modern movement, big names, less well-known names, people totally unknown, have been using this principle. I discovered this plastic freedom much later in life. Suddenly one has totally new possibilities, new horizons. Exterior or interiors, unity of inside and outside can be complete. This is not being aerodynamic, with the exception of tall buildings. Nature usually does not create aerodynamic shapes. Of course creativity here is made possible with the help of machines. Shapes and forms impossible to quantify in the recent past are now possible. The help of electronic or physical models is essential. Can we expect more and new forms of buildings? The first truly free-form city? After all, nature has been doing this for some time. Let's look around. Plastic freedom is liberation of the mind. Plastic freedom is magic.

'Rather sensuous, more like a female body in contrast to sharp-angled male architecture.' F. Kiesler

1. Socco chair. 2. Ushida Finlay. 3. A. Bruyere. 4. Y. Nogushi. 5. R. B. Fuller. 6. O. Niemeyer. 7. L. Baldessari. 8. A. Gaudi. 9. E. Mendelsohn. 10. Czech bunker.

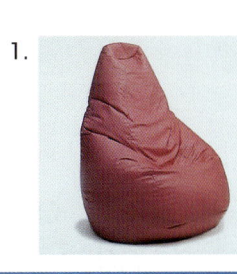
1.

2.

3.

4.
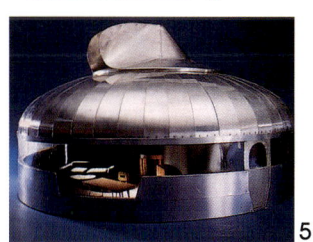
5.

6.

8.

9.

7.

10.

27

BEAUTY

It is astonishing how late I started to think about this thing – beauty. It was probably a reaction to there being more ugliness around. Ugliness and visual impotence is almost the norm for many. They do not see. They never show their faces in public. They just have heavy lunches. Let's not forget about all this. Let's search for beautiful things. Let's find astonishingly beautiful things – there are many of them around. Let's see the beauty. Let's see beautiful creatures. Life. Flowers. Trees. Water. Sun. Sky. Stars. Silence. A beach with pink sand. Let's admire that little island like a huge boulder, African trees like tall buildings. Structure of the tree. Structure of the single leaf. Creations of nature are always beautiful. Sitting on the beach is beautiful. That beautiful woman on the beach. Sitting in a Paris café with a drink. Sitting under a blue sky. Going bare-foot on the beach. The almost non-existent structure of a jellyfish. Let's see all of this. Many people do not. I feel sorry for them.

'Beauty governs all.' Le Corbusier

1. Sand. 2. Jellyfish. 3. Flower. 4. Beach. 5. Water. 6. Granite Island. 7. Baobab trees. 8. Pebbles.

BEAUTY

Two beauties, 25,000 years apart. One sculpture – one human being. We have the same feelings about them. Both are astonishingly beautiful, both have a simple, almost abstract form. It is magic to see both forms. We can be almost romantic about this. We can be sentimental. Beauty created by man and beauty created by nature. The endless beauty of the human body. The modern body, and even a body from several centuries back. The beauty of a moving body. The beautiful intimacy of a body – the first intimate touch. You can feel skin and you can smell it. We can think about our first date, our first love letter – written or received. There is no harm in being sentimental about it. Then there is the beautiful form of an African mask. The beauty of colours and power of Rothko painting. Moore sculpture, and its form. The totally abstract form of a Brancusi head. Totally complimentary to nature's creativity. Let's create beauty inspiration here. Let's use it. Beauty can be endless.

'Beauty is absolute.' A. Raymond

1. Body. 2. Body, 25,000BC. 3. Human spine. 4. I. Noguchi. 5. Foetus. 6. Modern body. 7. H. Moore. 8. African mask. 9. C. Brancusi.

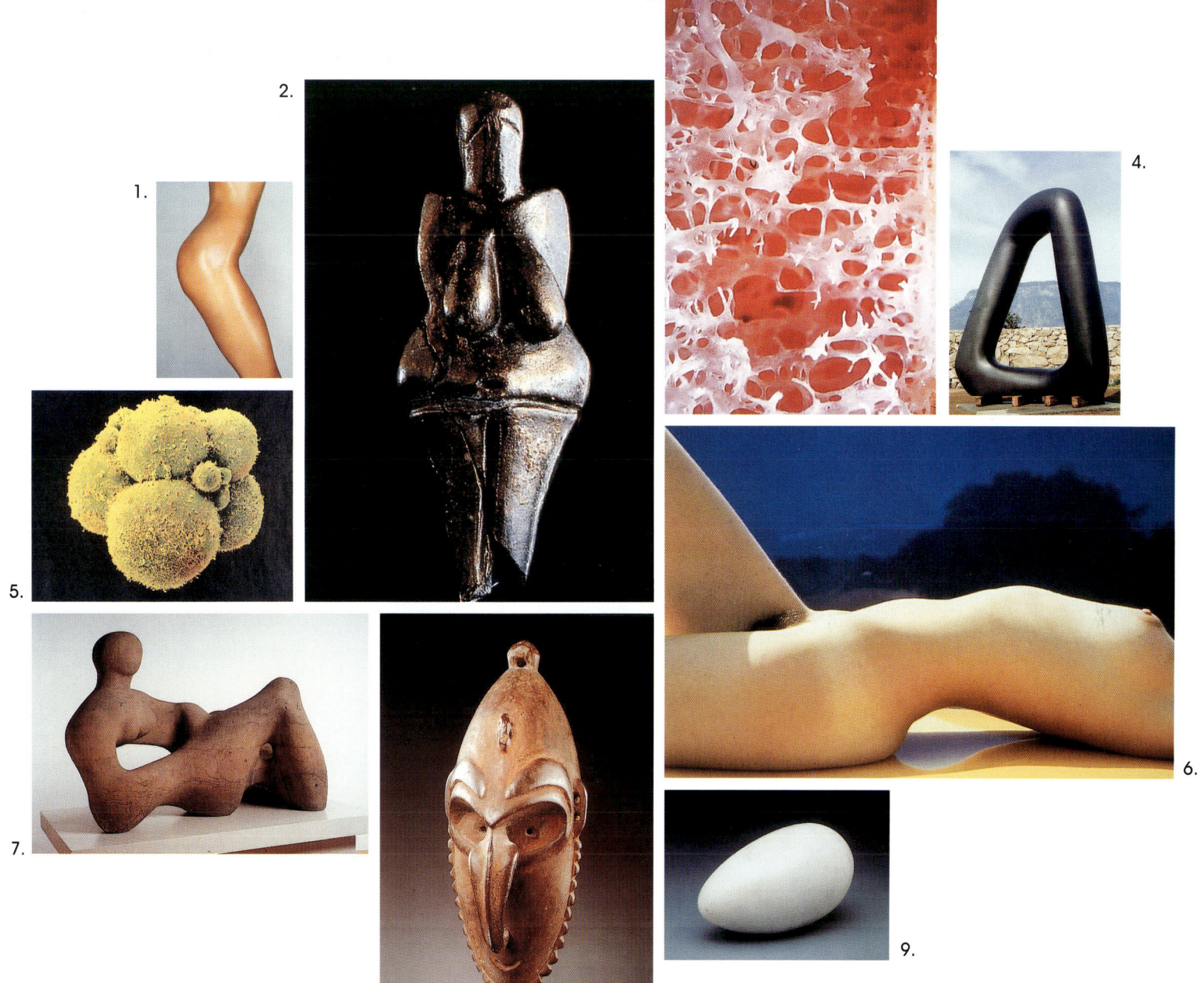

BEAUTY

Even man's creations can be astoundingly beautiful. Often they at least match those of nature. Both have one thing in common – they take one's breath away. Creations a thousand years old, a hundred years old, or only three years old, small or large. The hidden beauty of the microchip or silicon wafer. Nor in the case of an aeroplane is it all aerodynamics or structure. There are also the feelings of man behind it – the background and origin of the creator. The result may be utilitarian shape, but it is art as well. The creator here is not just engineer and human being, but artist. The product is so beautiful that it can easily sit not in a hangar but in an art gallery. Why is this process of creativity leading to beauty so alien in architecture? Here very few think of beauty, and architectural magazines are terrified to use the word. Architects do not talk about beauty. It is never mentioned as a target in the design process. Why is beauty almost a forgotten word? Let's change all this. Let's have more beauty around, especially in architecture. More and more.

'It serves no purpose other than that of beauty itself.' O. Niemeyer

1. FS Media Centre, London, 1995. 2. Circuit board. 3. Propeller, 1827. 4. Camera, 2001. 5. Shaver, 1960. 6. Proteus aeroplane, 1998. 7. Table, 1937. 8. Silicon wafer. 9. Apple iBook, 1999.

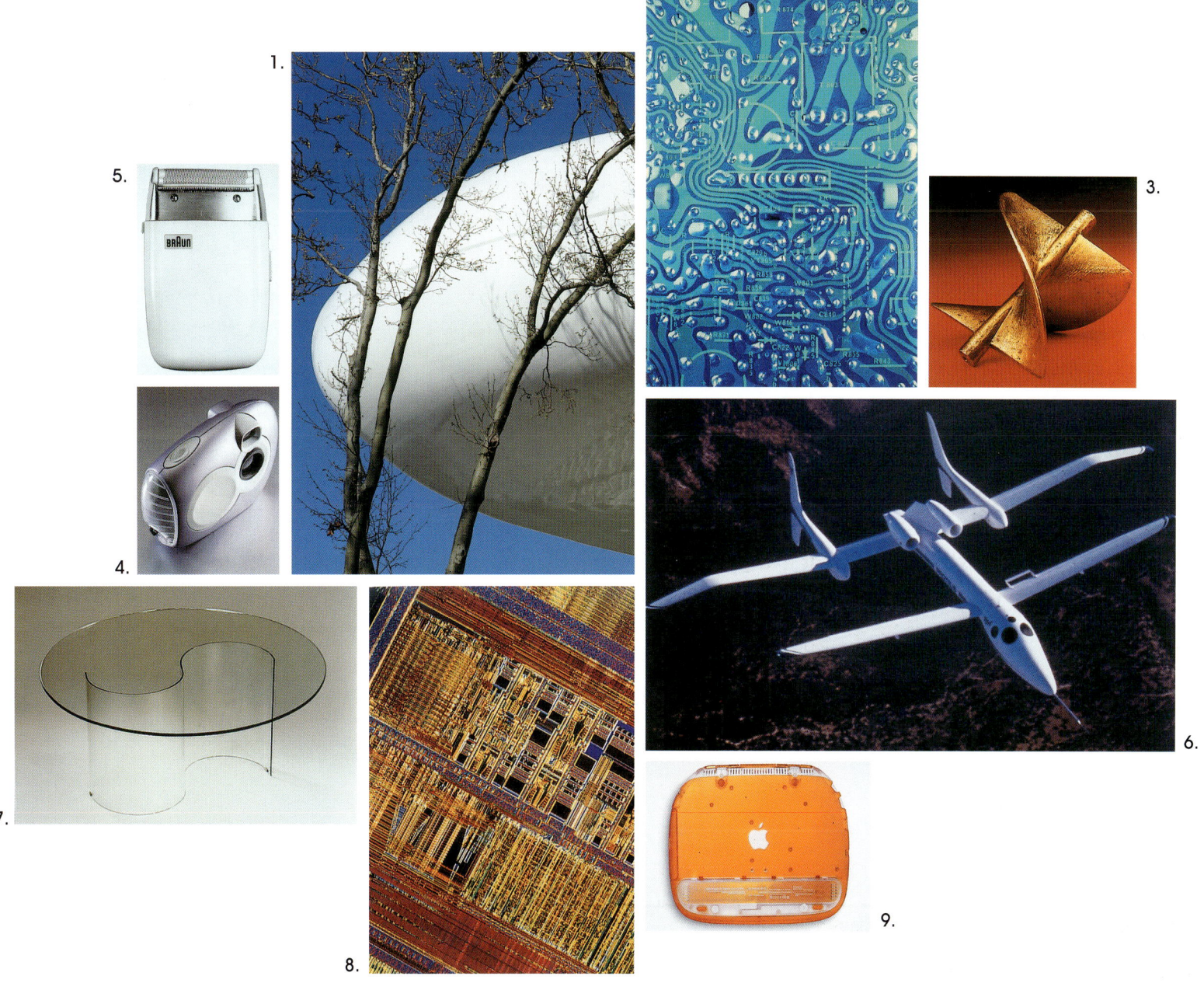

33

POETRY

Of course architecture must be poetic. All of it – inside and outside. The more gentle and poetic, the better it is. Small buildings, large buildings. Urban environment. Every building, especially inside, has many, many elements that can be poetic. In real poetry there are only words to be used. In architecture there is the whole building and the whole environment. Materials, colour, texture, light or shadow. We hardly use greenery as a poetic element. Its users should be gentle and poetic beings, not just the football crowd. Powerful prose can be poetry. Let's use this formula more often in architecture. Great architecture always was and always will be poetry. This is another dimension one should think about every day. Lots of architects do not do so at all. This is so much a neglected factor. Even the best examples of engineering are poetic. Above all, the flower and the blue sky are certainly poetic. Good architecture is always poetic.

'I think of dreams and poetry.' O. Niemeyer

1. Greek monastery. 2. Figure and screen. 3. Le Corbusier. 4. FS Marni shop, London, 1999. 5. Baily bridge, Italy. 6. A. Malraux 7. Conservatory, France. 8. Window, Spain. 9. Lavender field, France.

35

ELEGANCE

Elegance is also never spoken about. It is a critical element of good design or architecture. Yet it is more obvious on a pair of shoes or a beautiful dress. Maybe less obvious on something like a chair, elegant car or elegant bridge. Elegance is essential. Elegant building? Even more difficult. But it must be there. As always with these things, many people never think about it. Never achieve it. In many cases they never even try. Sometimes it comes to projects almost naturally. Sometimes via people who did not go to art or architectural school. Here we can see many striking examples. In nature there are hundreds. What is elegance? It is probably a combination of shape, colour, beauty, gentleness, expression and function. An elegant thing of the past is almost certainly elegant now. Let's create things that will remain elegant in the future. Many certainly will.

'Reason is the enemy of imagination.' M. Heidegger

1. 'Airline' armchair. 2. Ganter bridge. 3. Shoe and leg. 4. Glider. 5. 'Voyager' plane. 6. Ferrari F355 car. 7. Leaf. 8. Black dress. 9. Citroën car.

1.
2.
3.
4.
5.
6.
7.
8.
9.

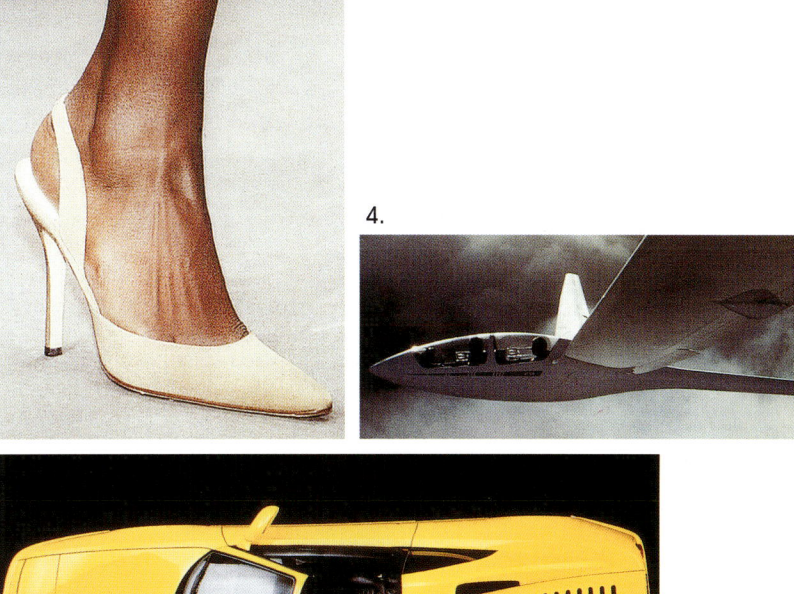

37

SENSUALITY

Sensuality of the tropical plant, light, skin, perfume, classical music, jazz, art…and much more. We are sometimes not aware of this richness around us. How to integrate all this into design should be critical. How to enrich interior and exterior. How to use natural or artificial light. How art should be totally incorporated within the space, not just added as a decoration. How smell can be something wonderful. How we can touch those soft, hard and perfumed walls. How we can experience completely new tastes in that space. How our skin can react. How we can kiss in this space. How we can make love. These form just the beginning of the design process. It could be almost magic. It could be that sensuality is the not yet explored fifth dimension. How people move through the space. How people move around the building. It is possible to introduce many of these sensual pleasures. How to make more people happy. Even more happy. This is just the start of the fifth dimension sensuality.

'We reduce art to its simplest expression which is love.'   A. Breton, 1924

1. Perfume. 2. Tropical plant. 3. F. Drtikol. 4. Finger. 5. Breast. 6. Music. 7. Mouth. 8. Net dress. 9. Skin.

1.
2.
3.
4.
5.
6.
7.
8.
9.

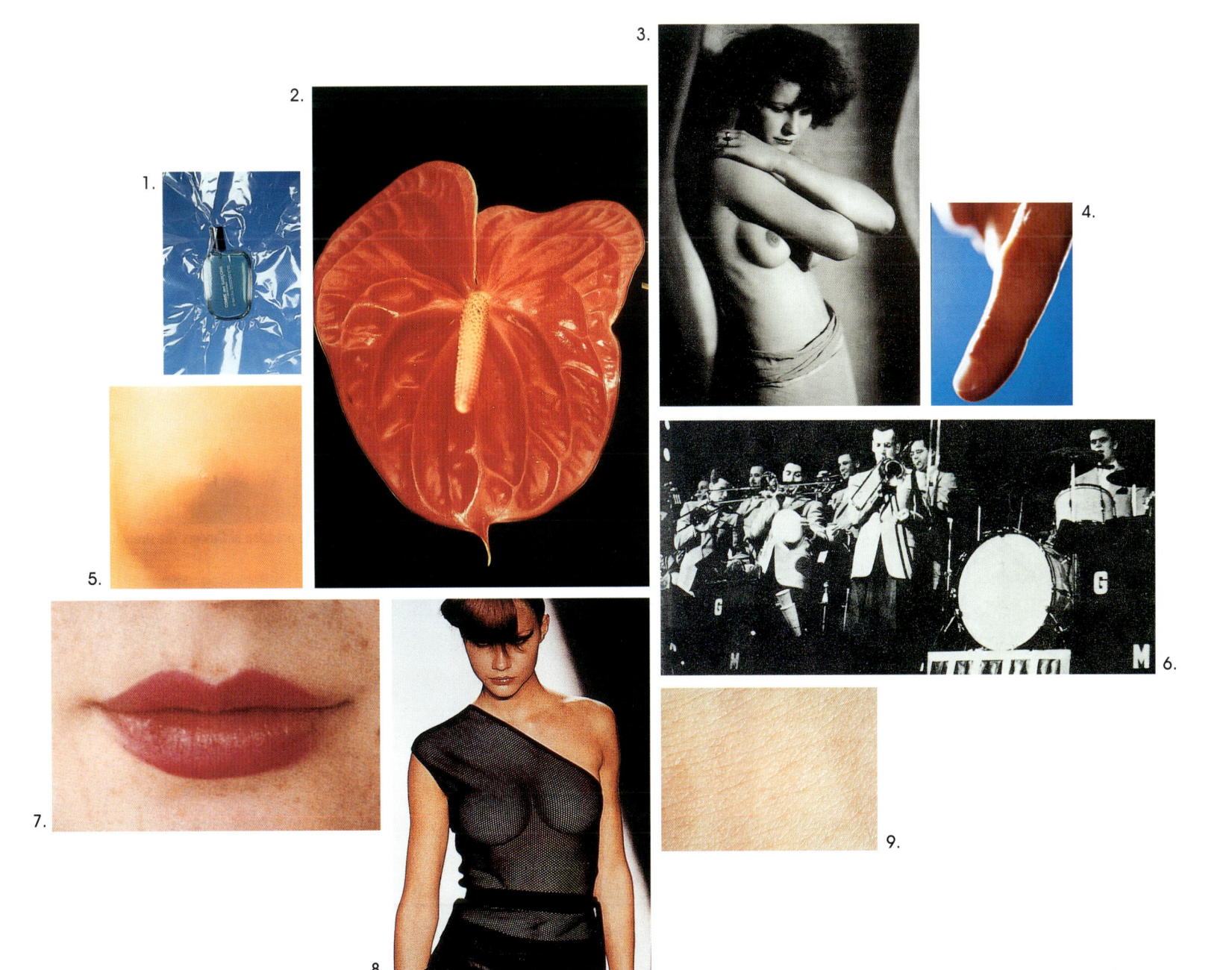

39

SEXUALITY

What is the magic final touch in any design? It must be sexuality – something that is difficult to describe in words. It is more of a feeling, almost a smell. It is that feeling of being on a first date. Who are the people who have managed to add this dimension to design? People have tried for generations. Sometimes it is gentle, recently more explicit. Eileen Grey's bedroom certainly has this feeling. Carlo Molino was openly interested. Niemeyer is drawing young ladies next to his creations – his building forms speak for themselves. Le Corbusier is naturally interested, as is evident in his drawings. Did his architecture truly change to become more curvy just because he met a certain young lady? We shall never know. Sexuality is accepted in all other art disciplines – painting, sculptures, photography, film and especially fashion. Why in architecture is it such a taboo subject? Why is it thought of as wrong? I think quite the opposite is true. There is not enough of it. Look at the thousands of buildings that have been conceived by people who never had a date or sex. One client said on seeing our design, 'It is sexy'. This was the highest compliment.

'But all art is erotic.' A. Loos

1. K. Molino. 2. Nineteenth-century dress. 3. Soap sculpture. 4. JK Photomontage, 1975. 5. A. Frey, R. Loewy. 6. E. Grey. 7. Twentieth-century dress. 8. L. Colani.

1.

2.

3.

4.

5.

6.

7.

8.

41

PEOPLE

People are without a doubt a crucial design element. They are certainly the first consideration in any design process. How different they are. How they have changed in the last year, last hundred years or last millennium. The form of their bodies. Even here there is noticeable change, for example they may be an inch taller. What do they think? How do they dress? How do they dream? It is almost impossible to comprehend how different they are even from those of only a generation before. The difference between men and women. The difference where children are involved. From loving couple to football hooligans. From marching soldiers to people on the beach. On the other hand, are they really that different from the people in photographs of the first modern buildings? In the third millennium some on this planet still live exactly as their predecessors 10,000 years ago – certainly a different lifestyle from most of us today. I cannot think about this all of the time. Let us think of contemporary people. Let us design for people.

'Reshape the environment, do not try to reshape man.' R. B. Fuller

1. Etruscan man. 2. Couple. 3. Soldiers. 4. Beach. 5. Amazon Indians, 2000. 6. Children. 7. Skinheads. 8. Miner.

1.

2.

3.

4.

5.

6.

7.

8.

43

PEOPLE

As architects we have to design for contemporary and future people. We need to visualise and think about what type of people will use the buildings and structures being designed today. It is truly difficult to visualise the people that will be around in the next 30 or 50 years. Though they will probably be very similar in looks, they will have very different needs. The needs of 'ordinary' people. The needs of presidents, monarchs and occasionally dictators. The needs of sportsmen and politicians still in eighteenth-century stockings. There will not be the 'universal' people who appeared on the pages of the Neufert or Metric handbook. Architects cannot dictate life to suit their drawings. They must investigate new forms of living and working. The modern movement is the first major contribution towards this. Healthier living for people. The new role of the kitchen, bathroom, auditorium, cinema, station and outdoor green space. Architects should listen to, and create for people, not ignore them. Photographs of their buildings are always without people. The main design element is missing – that cannot be right.

'Yes! The human body is the most extraordinary universe.' F. Kiesler

1. Presidents. 2. Football crowd. 3. House of Lords. 4. Female astronaut. 5. High society. 6. Dictator. 7. Monarch. 8. Hard hat.

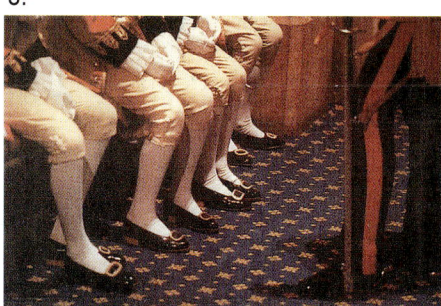

1.

2.

3.

4.

5.

6.

7.

8.

45

COLOUR

Even historically colour is one of the critical elements of any design. It is a major element in nature, where even gold, silver and fluorescent exist. It is only architects who have a problem with colour. They think black-and-white, then some of them add colour. Thousands of grey creations – inside and outside. Are these architects colour-blind? On the other hand, it is astonishing how colour comes naturally to many cultures. Bright, sophisticated, unusual colours – almost fluorescent. Architecture here has to learn also from art. It must learn from plants and animals. How refreshing it is to look at the work of Le Corbusier, Luis Barragan, Oscar Niemeyer, Richard Rogers and others. Colour is architecture. It is not added afterwards. Greek villagers paint their doors beautiful bright colours, and outstanding architecture can be seen here. There are the new colours of plastic materials. Is this lack of colour a development from the nineteenth century? Black-and-white publications in architectural schools? Can we change all this? We must. We need a more colourful future. Life is not only black-and-white. Only architecture sometimes is.

'Colour and me are one.' P. Klee, 1914

1. India. 2. M. Rothko. 3. Cambodia. 4. Baroque church. 5. India. 6. Tropical fish. 7. Coloured skin. 8. Rocks. 9. Moroccan boat.

1.
2.
3.
4.
5.
6.
7.
8.
9.

47

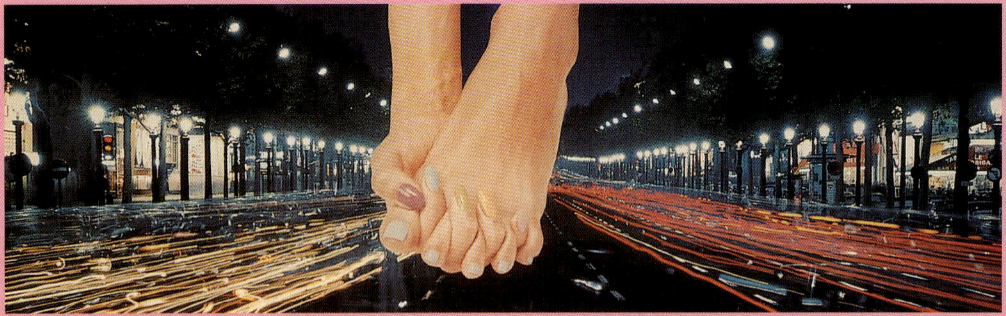

ARCHITECTURE

NEW PROFESSION

'There will be no architecture in fifteen years', said developer Mr Ron German in the year 2000. That is, in 2015. Mr German is of course fundamentally wrong. Architecture was here a thousand years ago and will be here in 3001 and for many years after. Everything is architecture, from the smallest paperclip, a shed, housing, church or museum, to major urban plans. It is quality, function and relationship to human beings on the planet Earth that are important – not scale. Architecture will not be replaced by functional sheds churned out on a Friday afternoon. Interest in architecture is growing. It doesn't matter if a couple of architectural writers think the same. People will always require architecture as a creative process and as part of their enhanced living. The future can hardly be predicted in a couple of sentences – only new reality can be the future.

'Who wants to look at boring pictures of buildings? They all look the same.'
J. Ritblat

1. 'Envisat' spacecraft. 2. Dolmen the Burren. 3. M. McLuhan. 4. Fashion. 5. Fifteenth-century church. 6. Mars landing. 7. Submarine bunks. 8. FS Boatel, London, 1990.

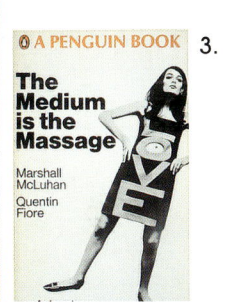

1.

2.

3.

4.

5.

6.

7.

8.

51

NEW PROFESSION

There must be a chance for a new profession – architecture with a new name and a new meaning. Space research started only fifty years ago. There was no tradition, no precedent – it simply did not exist. Only new targets, new people and some new technologies. But then came a new sense of how to serve people, a new sense of future and almost automatically new aesthetics – even new beauty. Looking forward there is certainly the need for new beauty, new reality. The new profession of architecture will be the profession of scientists, engineers and artists. It could quickly develop the confidence of progressive clients with its professional approach. The fragile line between science and art must be retained. Every developer now knows that good architecture sells. This can all be achieved without the interference of a few backward-looking people. The battle will be won onscreen or on the drawing board, not in a meeting room, Sunday newspaper or at a dinner party.

'There need be no "creative" or intellectual component to it at all.' M. Pawley

1. Pacemaker. 2. Antonio Sant'Elia. 3. M. Pawley. 4. Beautiful shed. 5. Sixteenth-century hall. 6. Old and new. 7. Aircraft. 8. Mass production.

53

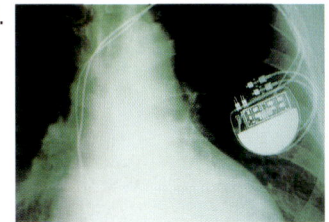

EUROPE

A new architectural identity is emerging. Europe. The home of old and longstanding architectural culture. After the disappearance of the US as an architectural power in early 1970s, Europe started to excel. This is now even more clear after 20 years of the dark ages of postmodernism. Look at the spiritual boom in European architecture. Every form, every system, every expression is tested. Even classicism is used, though only in Britain. European architects are building in other countries and other continents. Their imagination is used in the Far East, and now even in the US. The European cultural base is always evident. The contrast and drama of old and new is always around. Some European countries are emerging as strong architectural identities. Britain, France, Spain and Holland are almost architectural super powers. Europe is working together on many projects – space, aeroplanes, trains, cars, banknotes even postage stamps, and European architecture competitions. Let's use this pool of creativity in design architecture and urbanism. Will a European style emege? Will a European citizen-architect emerge? Europe must keep its architectural and cultural identity. Far East or US building practices are destroying European thinking. 'Pound in your pocket' is now an obsolete political slogan – no longer reality.

'Will Britain still exist in the year 3001?' A. C. Clarke

1. Provence, France. 2. London. 3. European Space Agency (ESA) Project. 4. Europe from above. 5. Perugia. 6. ESA magazine. 7. Stamp. 8. TGV train. 9. Prague. 10. Airbus project.

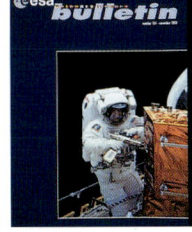

1.

2.

3.

4.

6.

5.

7.

8.

10.

9.

55

SOCIAL FACTOR

Modern architecture in the twentieth century started with raising and pointing out the need for better social conditions. Better and modern housing, schools and hospitals. Architects studied, wrote about, designed, and were sometimes allowed to build their answers to social problems in the battle for better living conditions for those on lower incomes. Healthier, new construction methods, new internal planning, new forms of urban planning and above all affordable rent systems. Certainly something was achieved, but people still live in unspeakable conditions, even in Europe. No running water, no bathroom, no heating, no ventilation and very limited daylight. Recently there has been very little architectural interest in this area. Architects are rarely asked to design new solutions. Many do not even dream of new solutions, and architectural magazines will probably not publish them anyway. Shelters for those who have absolutely no place to go is another area. I have tried several forms of emergency shelters, without a single sentence of support, and only childish criticism. These projects were never even published. Let's start a new chapter in the third millennium. Let's increase interest in the social factors of architecture.

'20% of adults in Britain are illiterate and innumerate.' Labour Party Report, 1997

1. Social housing, Austria. 2. Public space. 3. Salvation Army boat. 4. Brazil, 2001. 5. Britain, 2001. 6. FS Shelter, 1985. 7. Britain, 2001. 8. France, 2001.

1.

2.

3.

4.

8.

6.

5.

7.

CULTURE

Why has architecture always battled for its position as a part of cultural life? For many 'architects' this statement does not mean much. For many people, architecture is the putting together of bricks. Alternatively, it is being the developer or estate agent. This is not so. Architecture's prime function is to be part of culture. Architecture must contribute to people's lives. It can enhance their lives. It can create better working and living conditions. Above all, architecture can create a beautiful environment, beautiful building, something to look at and live in with pleasure. Green spaces, town squares, streets with blue sky, snow, clouds – the composition is complete. Architecture is a culture. Culture is not complete without architecture. There are thousands of examples where buildings are not part of culture, not even conceived as part of culture. This is certainly because culture is not part of the thinking of their 'creators'. But they are responsible. They are the guilty party.

'There are 100 million kids who never go to school.' B. Clinton

1. Charles Bridge, Prague. 2. IBM building, New York. 3. M. Kundera. 4. Entrance ticket for Centre Pompidou, Paris 5. L. Barragan. 6. Centre Pompidou, Paris. 7. Daniel Buren, Paris, 1986. 8. Stamp. 9. H. Moore, Zurich.

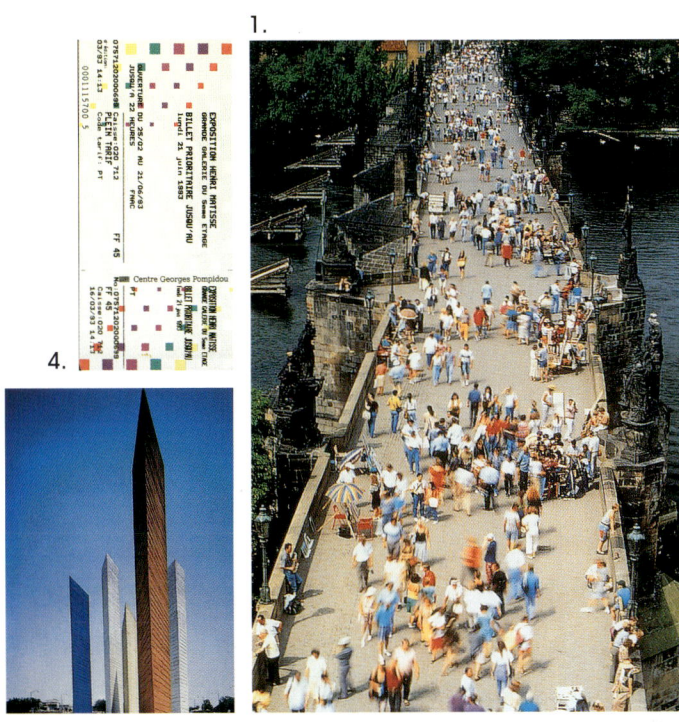

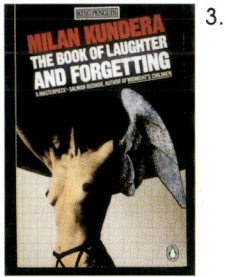

1.

2.

3.

4.

5.

6.

7.

8.

9.

POLITICS

In my life I have been through six years of fascism and twenty years of communism. That is plenty. Too much. Both have a disastrous effect on anybody's architectural creativity. Dogma after dogma. Political not architectural thinking. People destroyed. Buildings destroyed. No criticism allowed, no serious publications permitted. Nationalism was in great evidence, classicism as architectural form. No room, will or need for independent thinking. Even in a democratic state, any political party or group simply cannot dictate political solutions in architecture. Politicians usually have no interest in or knowledge of these matters. The creative process in art or architecture is far more sophisticated than political dogma or speeches. The French know this well. Malraux or Lang are first seen as intellectuals, then politicians. When I hear that architects are elitist by one political party, I despair. Interest from Royals can be even more dogmatic and political. More creativity than politics is essential.

'The great blessing of the global age is the explosion of democracy.' B. Clinton

1. Africa's conflict. 2. Northern Ireland's conflict. 3. *Perspectives* magazine. 4. Fascist dome. 5. Communist dome. 6. North Korea. 7. Tate Modern, London. 8. Modern transport. 9. Old transport.

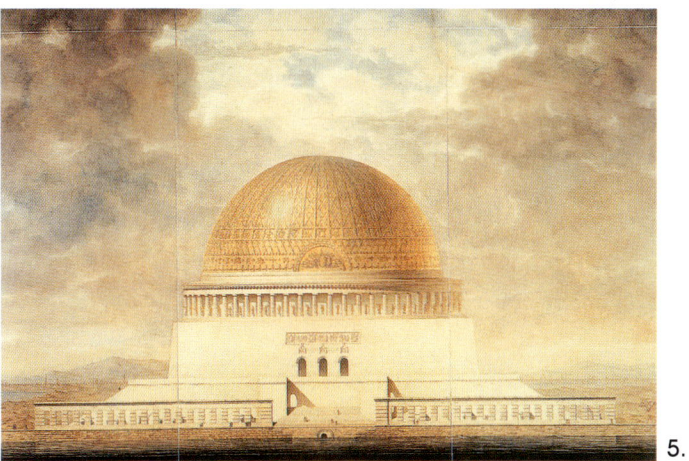

1.

2.

3.

4.

5.

6.

7.

8.

9.

61

FROM ABOVE

Antoine de Saint-Exupery, his books, his Little Prince, his thoughts, his survivals, his spirit and his mysterious end – all this means something to me. Quite a lot. It is this type of spirit that architects need most. There is not enough flying in architecture. Walking along a dusty road is not good for new spirited thoughts. One can always think more freely while flying. Some attempts at flying are crushed even on take-off. Some things are dismissed before even being explained. Let's see things in perspective. Let's see a few years ahead. Let's be interested in new dimensions. The possibilities are endless. Look at the fabulous aerial photographs, from an airship only 200 metres above or a satellite more than 50,000 metres above. They bring a totally new dimension. New hope. The world looks different from above. More exciting, maybe more promising. Architects and planners could not see all this just a few years ago. Our new buildings should match this amazing spectacle. It is obvious from above that buildings and urban planning is a totally three-dimensional world. It is not just a series of elevations and plans. According to Le Corbusier, viewing things from above brings a fourth dimension. Of course he was right. What a challenge here. From above.

'The aeroplane has unveiled for us the true face of the earth.' A. de Saint-Exupery

1. Irrigation system. 2. Radar altimeter surface. 3. A. de Saint-Exupery. 4. FS Wales house, 1994. 5. Potez XXV. 6. Airship dining-room. 7. Stamp. 8. FS Media Centre, London, 1995. 9. Le Corbusier. 10. Prague.

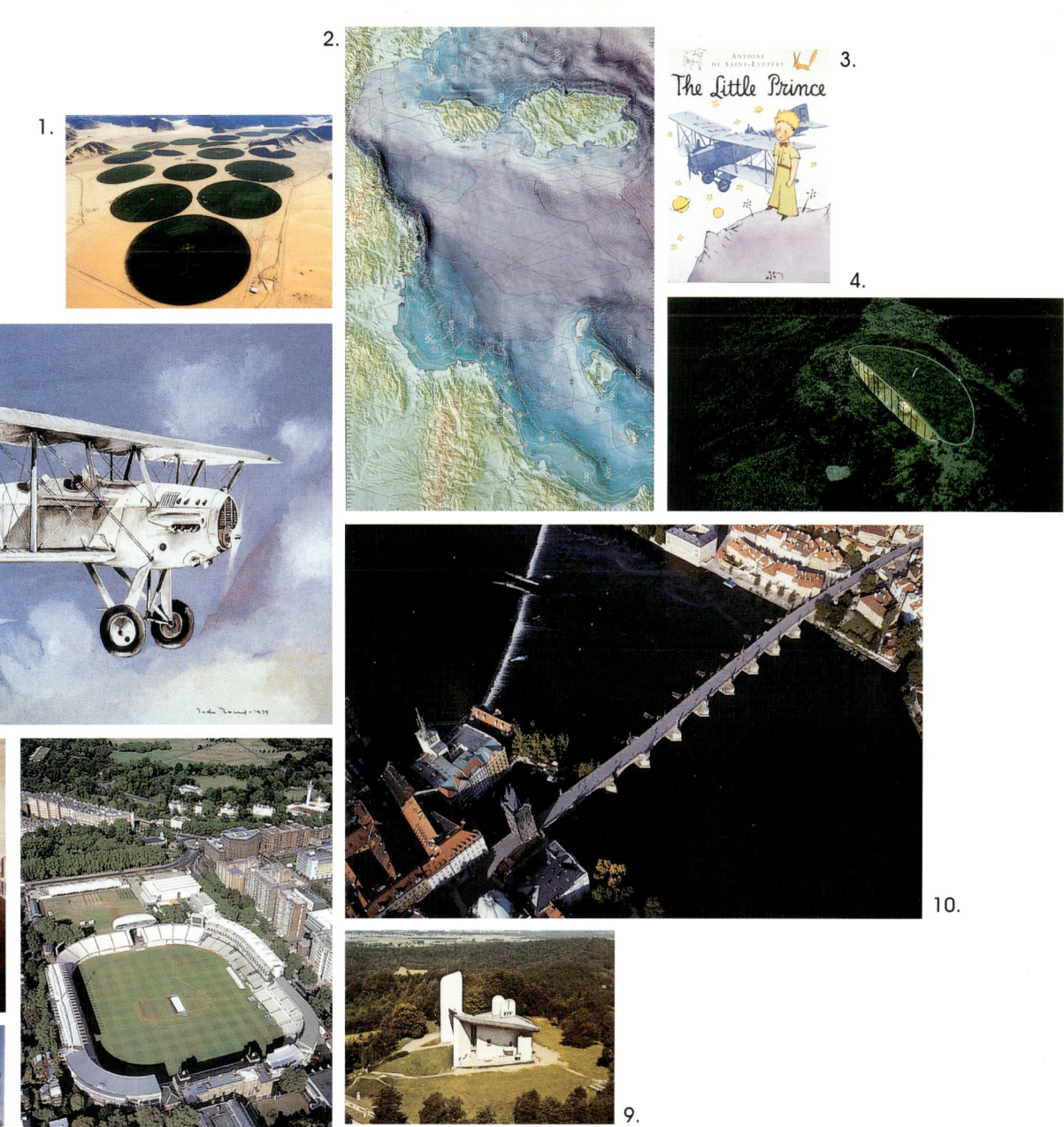

1.

2.

3.

4.

5.

6.

7.

8.

9.

10.

63

DISTANCE

People can now travel thousands of miles in a few hours. No intermediate landings are necessary. No sickness bags. Onboard the QEII it took five days to cross the Atlantic. On Concorde it takes two-and-a-half hours. It will be an hour in a few years time. We take all this for granted. You can reach friends, lovers, fellow professionals, meetings, conferences or lectures anywhere, in a maximum of 12 hours. The cost of this is going down all the time. Even cargo moves fast, in helicopters, in containers, or even in submarines. It is particularly visible in Europe, where borders are disappearing. Except in the heads of outdated politicians. You can go from London to Paris by train. No customs, no border guards. And you are going fast at over 300km per hour – almost the speed of a propeller-driven aeroplane. Vertical take-off or intercity helicopter travel must be the next step. Perhaps individual flying platforms after that. What an opportunity for architects to see, examine, study and contribute towards, for the benefit of future generations. I am always deeply touched to see hoards of young people travelling. They will not fight each other in new wars. The Iron Curtain did not survive for the same reasons. Neither will future dictatorships survive. Potentially truly international architecture.

'The aeroplane revealed everything to us.' Le Corbusier

1. Submarine. 2. Queen Elizabeth II. 3. Crane helicopter. 4. VTOL V-22 aeroplane. 5. Super Sonic Transport plane. 6. TGV train. 7. Crane helicopter. 8. Container ship. 9. Young people.

1.

2.

3.

4.

5.

6.

7.

8.

9.

65

EVOLUTION

Architecture is an extremely static profession. A few believe there is a need to go further with buildings – not artificially in terms of styles. Despite the fact that there is an enormous need for evolution, sometimes revolution in architecture, in reality there is almost zero evolution. There is no evolution in housing, and even upmarket apartment blocks have changed very little in the last 75 years. Only equipment has changed. Heating ventilation, kitchen and bathroom fittings – future tenants are forced to take them or leave them. There is not enough architectural spirit here. If you stay in any hotel room you are frustrated by impotent room and bathroom layouts. Will somebody design practical, efficient and beautiful hotel rooms? What about large buildings? Office blocks have changed only in elevation, with the internal arrangements remaining exactly the same for decades. Even the computer revolution did not touch basic layout. And what about even larger buildings? Stations, airports, cinemas, car parks – there is a massive need for evolution here. New and experimental solutions must come from architects. They will never come from developers or governments. Look at the progress in other professions in the last hundred years – there is a lesson here. The spirit and bravery of Santos-Dumont and the Wright Brothers should be introduced in architecture. It must be.

'A moon base the size of a small village by 2020.' BT Laboratories

1. Modern balloon, 1998. 2. Space flight, 1953. 3. Modern glider, 1990. 4. Montgolfier hot-air balloon. 1783. 5. Santos-Dumont, 1905. 6. B-2 stealth bomber, 1989. 7. Horten HVII stealth bomber, 1945. 8. Space flight, 2000. 9. Lilienthal glider, 1896.

1.

3.

2.

4.

5.

6.

7.

8.

9.

67

KITSCH

To put a classical dome on top of a supermarket is not just kitsch, it is a crime. This has previously been done in the Central African Republic. Hitler and Stalin used the dome as well. It is now used by distinguished members of the architectural profession who cannot see the primitivism of it. They also have eyes. Yet it seems they do not know how to use them. They are visually blind. They would probably do anything for money. They probably never read the book. They are almost always dressed correctly in grey suits with grey ties and grey socks. They just destroy the beautiful world around them. There are thousands of them around the world. Their wives always wear Laura Ashley dresses. They have three hour lunches. Sometimes they even study architecture. Some have diplomas in architecture. They are certainly members of distinguished architectural bodies. They have lots of power. Yet they support and understand only ugliness. They create only kitsch. But let's ignore them. Totally.

'Ornament and crime.' A. Loos

1. Supermarket. 2. Cuckoo clock. 3. Children's book. 4. Monument. 5. Royal Gate, London. 6. Restaurant. 7. Chair. 8. Cup.

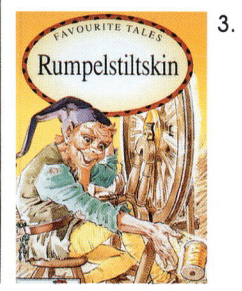

1.

2.

3.

4.

5.

6.

7.

8.

69

ECO

Nature is a master of ecological systems. Even tiny termites know how to build a well-tempered environment. Men have tried to follow only thousands of years later. For generations there was no interest, no need. Need is here now. The hole in the ozone is on my mind daily. Need is megatons of garbage. Need is millions of polluting cars, trains, buses, aeroplanes. Polluting buildings, everywhere. Polluting cement, steel production. Polluting obsolete power stations. Polluting obsolete heating systems and obsolete air-conditioning systems. Need is everywhere. Need is not to use lakes and rivers as dumping grounds. Need is to protect woods destroyed everywhere. Smog over every large city in the world. People getting sick, and 24,000 people in Britain dying prematurely. There is no, or very little interest from Downing Street and only aggressive negativism from the White House. No interest from Buckingham Palace. Absolutely no interest from major architectural practices. Absolutely no interest from potential clients.

'24,000 people die prematurely in Britain every year of air pollution.'
Newspaper, 2000

1. Beach, 2001. 2. Woods. 3. Ozone hole. 4. Windmill. 5. Power station. 6. Garbage dump. 7. Roof screen. 8. Electric car (105km/h), 1899. 9. Termite nest.

71

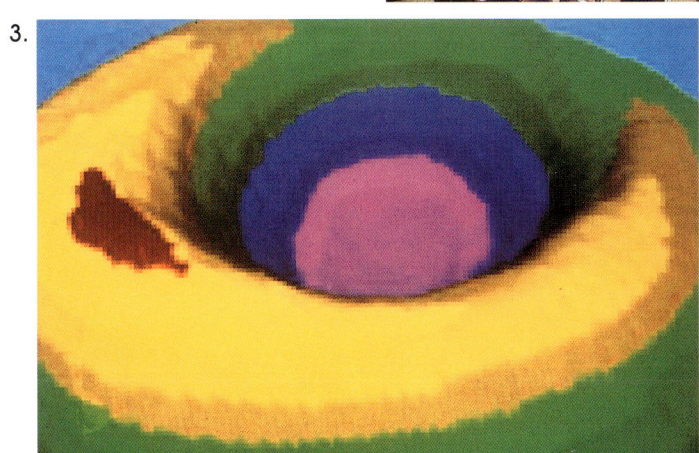

ECO

There is amazing beauty in a field of slowly moving propellers of windmill generators. Beauty of purpose. Beauty of giant sculptures. Beauty of something new. A true indication of the third millennium. An indication of things to come. The vertical generator is of course another future development. The possibility of buildings generating almost 100 per cent of their energy needs. Future Systems has already designed one. A tall office building in an urban environment with a vertical generator. The use of generators and solar cells will become prime elements of new architecture. These elements will not be added, they will be the architecture of future buildings. A new eco form. What about the green car? Its evolution is not supported. Development is almost non-existent. Progress since the first electric car of 1899 has been limited. It is fantastic to see in action the Eco buses of Paris, Vienna and the US. There has been very little research in the field of underwater turbines. Only beautiful illustrations exist. There are no tidalwave barriers either. With thousands of miles of coast this is impossible to understand. There has been no research into the task of beaming sun energy from outer space. Again only illustrations. Research into green materials is essential – the value of materials in green efficiency. There is no government support here either. No commercial incentive. This must become a government incentive and priority. Unlimited supply of cheap oil from the Middle East might not be so certain after 11 September 2001. But the ozone hole is here and getting bigger.

1. 10 Downing Street. 2. Solar chimney. 3. Vertical windmill generator. 4. Green bus. 5. Electric car. 6. Underwater generator. 7. Solar cells. 8. Vertical windmill generator. 9. FS Green Bird, London, 1996. 10. Dish collector.

73

GREEN SPACE

Why is green space such a totally underestimated, almost ignored element in architecture? Is it due to impatience with growing plants? Is it the impossibility to see green space completed within one's lifetime? It is more than this. Perhaps a lack of appreciation of the beauty of greenery. It is astonishing how many architects see greenery only as funny curly lines on their drawings – elements they cannot fully control. But greenery can be a compliment to a building. It can almost be a leading element, or the entire architecture of the building. There are astonishing examples around. The obvious beauty, scale and unique composition of the Japanese garden. The cubistic and formal layout of the Villa Noailles garden. The totally formal layout of the baroque garden. The natural composition of the Burle Marx gardens where the use of pebbles and boulders is magic. Then there is the use of water and a few trees at Paley Place in New York. The astonishing elegance of the gardens of Thomas Church. Generally very, very little is happening in this field. I wish I could make a contribution here, even a tiny one. Maybe one day. But it would be impossible for me to see it completed. That would be too late for me.

'The garden is transition between architecture and landscape.' B. Marx

1. Museum of Modern Art garden, New York, 1966. 2. London green space. 3. Garden and pool, Sonoma, 1948. 4. Villa Noailles garden, 1925. 5. Ryoan-Ji garden, eighteenth century. 6. San Cristobals Stables, 1967. 7. Cavanelas Garden. 8. Jardin Japonais, 1956. 9. Paley Place, New York. 10. Case study house 21, 1958.

1.
2.
3.
4.
5.
6.
7.
8.
9.
10.

75

STRUCTURE

Where is the evolution of structures heading? Controlled deflection, minimising sizes, and possibly few 'new materials'? Weight will certainly feature more heavily on the agenda. Some structures might be half of the weight of those today. The production and volume of the materials used is certainly related to pollution. So choice of materials might be affected by legal requirements. Some structures will tend towards the semi-monocoque used today in the boat and aeroplane industries. More and more inspiration will be drawn from nature. The use of computers will naturally help this process. Building codes will be broken and rewritten. Few people will panic at this evolution. What an exciting time will be to come. Maybe a new profession of artist-engineer-scientist will be born. Structure will be totally integrated with architecture – one new profession. Not the burden created by others that one must deal with later. Architects, engineers and artists will go to the same bar.

'If you think about voids instead of working with elements, truth appears.' N. Ricolais

1. Bridge, India. 2. Yacht mast. 3. Metro tunnel. 4. Fuselage section. 5. Aeroplane wing. 6. Parachute. 7. Le Corbusier's diagram. 8. Roof disk. 9. Train body.

77

STRUCTURE

The division here between brainwork and production will always remain. This is a critical point. The brain makes the first decision, then the machine takes over. With this combination man is capable of producing structures never before envisaged, even using existing materials and especially using new ones. Traditional materials will be used in new ways. Some older principles and formulas will go. Post and beam structures will be used more and more sporadically. Membrane structures, inflatable structures, new forms of skeletons. Lightness and transparency will be more present, after all nature does not use a post and beam structure. Nature uses materials in the most sophisticated and economical way. Weight ratio is often astonishing. Let's learn from that. With more and more sophisticated programmes available, and by using them at the right time it is possible. It is sometimes surprising how few architects are interested in this evolution. Quite often they only pretend to be interested.

'A building system of tensions in free space'. F. Kiesler

1. Car frame. 2. Skeleton. 3. Brassiere. 4. Kevlar yacht. 5. Grid dome. 6. Tent. 7. Bridge suspension. 8. Stainless steel membrane roof.

79

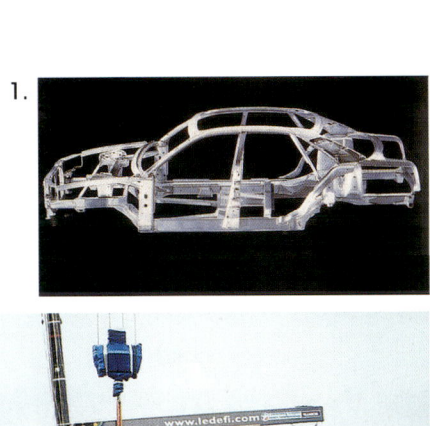

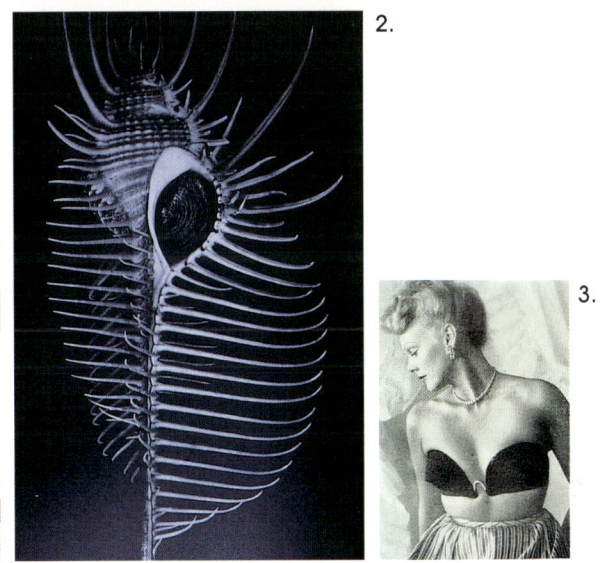

MATERIAL

Choice of material must be an experience of quality, durability, suitability, and probably also cost. Grassed banks or almost pre-historic stone. The tradition of wood. The flexibility of steel. The new possibilities of aluminium. The prospects of new advanced concrete. Sculptural forms in white concrete. Much later will come the introduction of carbon-fibre in buildings. Extraordinary new developments and the three-dimensional use of glass. The introduction of colour fritting in glass. The possibility of 'universal' structural and non-combustible material. Probably the real material of the future can go even further. There may be lessons from nature in composition and strengths. Lessons from nature in efficiency in the use of materials. How will these discoveries be used? There is the whole question of green sustainable materials. Green in production, transport and use. The question of the useful recycling of material. How can building codes be satisfied? New codes? New forms of testing? Yet new materials are never the only factor of progress in architecture. Only in harmony with concept and artistic talent can beautiful results be achieved.

'Efficiency of umbrella and bicycle.' R. B. Fuller

1. Velcro fibres. 2. Aluminium, carbon-fibre, titanium. 3. Abalone shell. 4. Stone wall. 5. Polyester fabric. 6. Ceramic tiles. 7. Earth bank. 8. Golden orb weaver spider. 9. Thermal insulation.

1.

2.

3.

4.

5.

6.

7.

8.

9.

81

PLANT

Plants are not abstract shapes or forms. They are living organisms. They are not just roses in suburban gardens. Not just part of a flowerbed. Not just a decorative pattern in public parks. Plants are mechanisms, living sculptures of astonishing beauty. They are colourful paintings. Sources of powerful smells. Gentle shadow. Structural miracles. Simple grass cut like best carpet, or more sophisticated grasses. Grass and boulders. Ivy fields. Bamboo trees of exceptional strength. Gentle larch trees. Evergreen umbrella pines. Pink magnolias, conical cypresses. The height of a solitary palm tree. A hornbeam hedge. Incredible three-dimensionally formed cacti. Or orchids highlighting sophisticated dress. How can one use all this natural richness? As a beautiful element. As a contrast. As a background. As a complement to a beautiful and new building. As calmness in the middle of a hostile environment. Let's use plants. Let's cover whole buildings. Green buildings. This must be more creative than another pile of concrete or steel. It adds a growing and live component. A magnificent architectural component. Plant.

'The plant is, above all things, dynamic. Its changes prove it is alive.' B. Marx

1. Grass, moss and stone. 2. Cypress tree. 3. Pine tree. 4. Ivy. 5. Palm tree. 6. Cacti. 7. Magnolia tree. 8. Moss and gravel. 9. Bamboo tree. 10. Cacti.

1.
2.
3.
4.
5.
6.
7.
8.
9.
10.

83

DETAIL

'God is in detail'. From one-off detail created by craftsmen many centuries ago to the mass-production detail of today. Detail created by nature. Detail by man. Classical detail. Early modern detail. Car production detail. Aeroplane and ship detail. Architectural detail. Furniture detail. Detail in wood, stone, aluminium, steel or carbon-fibre. Detail of bamboo stems. Detail of leaf ribs. Detail of skeletons. Future Systems detail. Mies's detail. Different styles of detail. Detail following the nature of material, beautiful concept detail. An outrageous detail. Good concept and bad detail. Detail as a concept. Detail for new material. Detail easy to draw and impossible to make. Beautiful or ugly detail. Bad detail. Simple detail. Detail one would like to touch. Detail of stitching, riveting, bolting, welding or folding. Colourful detail. Thinking of detail, creating detail. Revolutionary detail. No detail. Fashionable detail. Yes, I am talking about the same thing. Detail in design and architecture.

'God is in the detail.' L. Mies van de Rohe

1. Air intake. 2. Zip. 3. Human eye. 4. Garden. 5. Glazing. 6. Dashboard. 7. Bamboo boarding. 8. Car switch. 9. Dress. 10. Trainer.

85

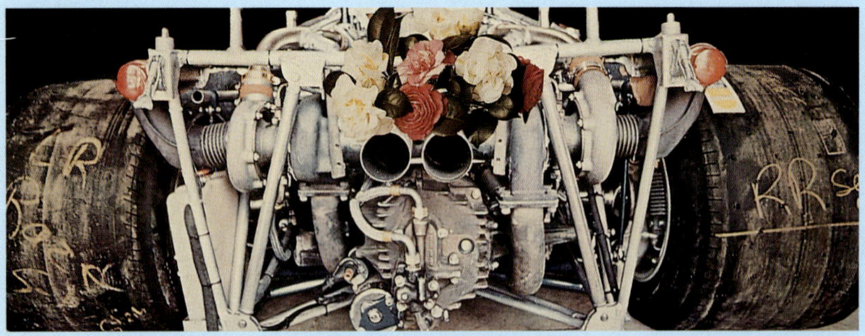

PROCESS

PROCESS

This is a process of discovery. Process is very primitive on the surface. Very personal. A piece of plasticine from the toy shop. A piece of polystyrene from the model shop. Two principal methods. Using hands, file and sand paper. Form-finding in the most simple way. Yet very quickly one can see the form. Already to scale. Always a simple sketch beforehand. One's spine shivers when a new form is emerging. No 'proper' drawings or sketches can so quickly discover the form. Mistakes can be quickly rectified. Forms impossible to draw are easily materialised. Then there are bigger and better models. Mock-ups. Hundreds of drawings on computer. Five computer form-finding programs in the case of the Media Centre. Almost every square inch of the surface is mapped. The final form has arrived. Several systems work together. It is naive to claim that just one button needs to be pressed. Maybe buttons are pressed 25,000 times. Nothing arrives easily. This is a process, not the stroke of a pen or pencil. Sometimes emotional and sentimental.

'There will be no architecture in 15 years.' R. German, 2000

1. FS Selfridges Building, 1999. 2. FS Selfridges building, Birmingham, 1999. 3. FS Coffee pot, 1996. 4. FS Bibliotheque National, Paris, 1989. 5. FS Green Building, London, 1990. 6. FS Media Centre, London, 1994. 7. FS Green Bird, London, 1996. 8. FS Bibliotheque National, Paris, 1989.

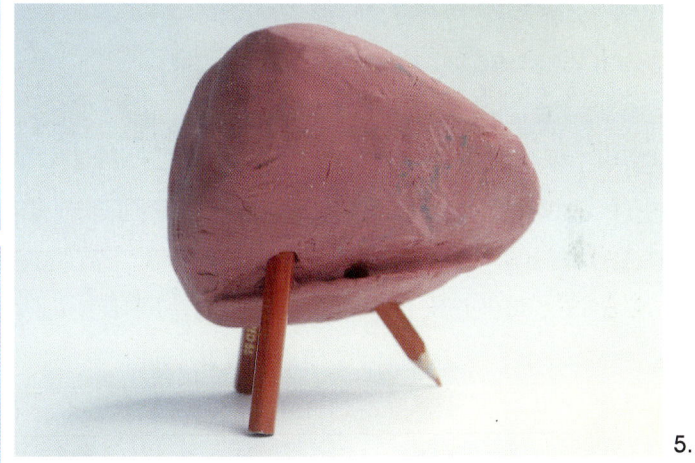

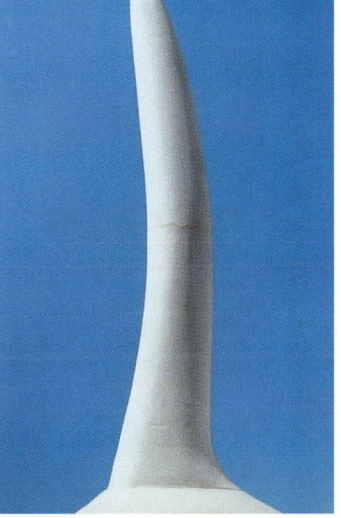

1.

2.

3.

4.

5.

6.

7.

8.

89

INFLUENCES

Yes of course there are influences. Some of them stronger than others. Some of them longer lasting, some of them disappearing. Sometimes represented by a direct link, sometimes more complicated. It is fascinating how one can be influenced even by little things, invisible things. Sometimes a principal lifetime influence. Influences from personal interests or the people around us. Influences from other architects. Details or whole concepts. Fashion is certainly an influence for its creativity and avalanche of new ideas, uncompromising vision and for looking forward. Influence from books, particularly biographies, autobiographies. Even a novel can sometimes be influential. Nature is a particularly strong influence and limitless inspiration, especially in form and advanced structure. Art is also a major source of influence. Freedom of artistic thinking and freedom of form are the envy of most architects. Sometimes jazz or chamber music written 300 years ago in candlelight yet still powerful and moving today. And structures of course. To understand the logic and almost coolness of their creators is vital for architects. But above all this, is the influence of a few good friends.

'I keep inside myself, in my private museum, everything I have seen and loved in my life.' A. Malraux

1. Architecture. 2. People. 3. Literature. 4. Technology. 5. Nature. 6. Art. 7. Fashion. 8. Music.

1.

2.

3.
Saint-Exupéry
Courrier sud

4.

5.

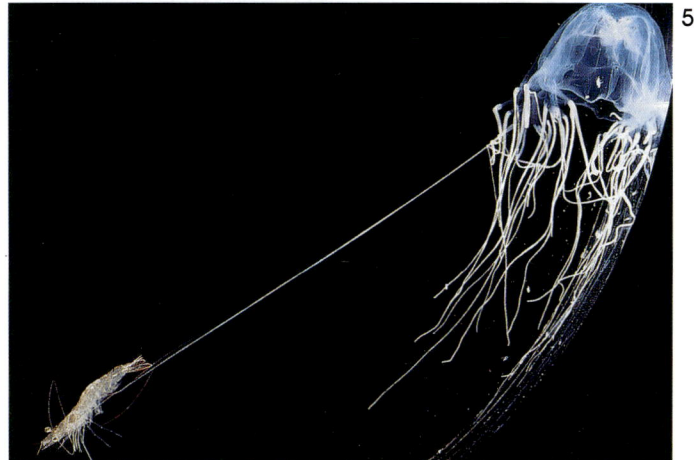

6.

7.

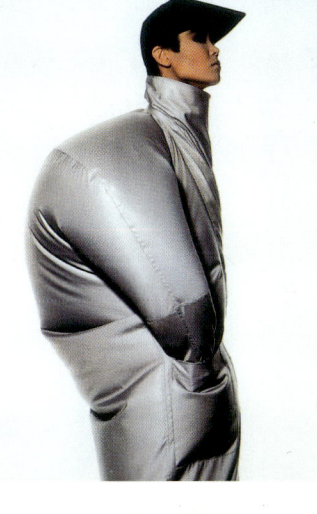

8.

91

DIALOGUE

One of the critical factors in any architectural design process is dialogue – personal contact. Exchange of ideas in cafés, restaurants or bars, particularly in the bar. Belonging to the same movement, the same table, has all but disappeared. Anglo-Americans were never very strong in movements. But you can visualise those heated discussions in Paris, Vienna and Zurich. Finally a manifesto is produced, and published. Private meetings between architects are almost unheard of now. There are still a few letters going around the world, people still read magazines and newspapers. But fax and email have brought about a complete revolution in communications. In a few moments written and printed documents can be exchanged. Fax still has the personal touch in the logo at the top. Email is another, completely impersonal matter – it does not even have a signature and it is impossible to know the country of origin. Meanwhile, exhibitions are gaining importance. It is a real pleasure to see a good architectural exhibition. To see the whole process of design on display. I hope they will not disappear. Human contact is still more important than any electronic device – the colour of somebody's eyes still matter. Let's be in touch. Let's have more dialogue.

'It always makes sense to tell the truth.' V. Havel

1. Exhibition. 2. Conversations. 3. Magazine. 4. Café. 5. Postcard. 6. Café. 7. Pleasure. 8. Newspapers. 9. Letter. 10. Airmail.

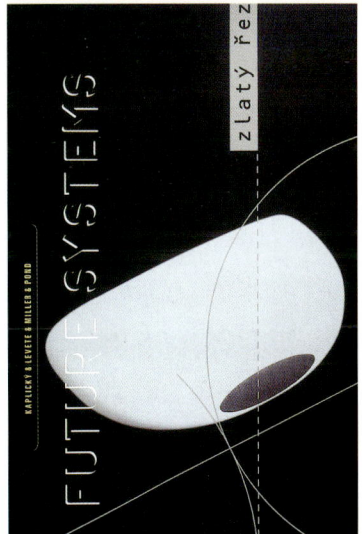

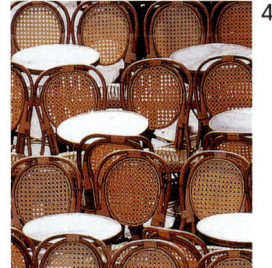

1.

2.

3.

4.

5.

6.

7.

8.

9.

10.

93

ANONYMOUS CREATORS

We all have our personal preferences. My interest here started a long time ago. Structures from different periods, different parts of the world. Sophisticated, 'primitive', big or small in scale. From different cultures, old or new. But they have one thing in common – they are honest. They do not have 'style'. They are above any fashion. They can be timeless. And because of all this they are beautiful, sometimes even poetic. This is why I like them. Many people, even many architects, cannot see this. It would never occur to them. They are not interested. The creators of these structures created in need, for pleasure, in belief, with knowledge. Even a bunker finished in three days in remote countryside is remarkable. They did not think of money. They did not think of time. But they created in many cases timeless objects, structures. Here is a sophisticated lesson for all of us as architects. Think of those whom we shall never know their names – anonymous creators.

'All is architecture.' H. Hollein

1. Cotton harvester. 2. Sails. 3. Bunker. 4. Chapel. 5. Terraces. 6. Stone house. 7. Ribbon bridge. 8. Teapot. 9. Ice gun. 10. Bollard. 11. Huts. 12. Aircraft carrier.

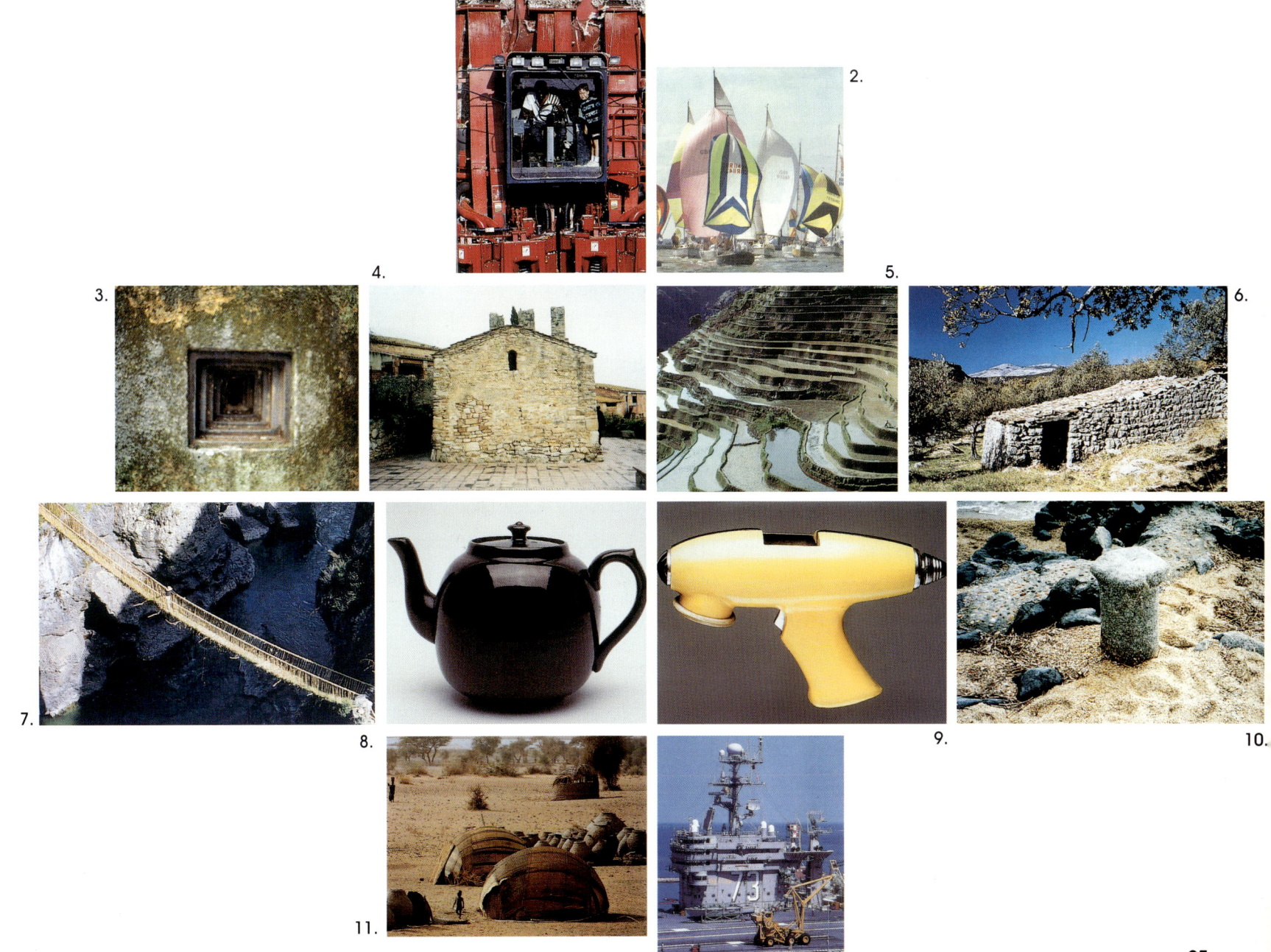

1.

2.

3. 4. 5. 6.

7. 8. 9. 10.

11. 12.

95

CONFUSION

Architecture or the design process can lead to complete historical, emotional, practical, visual or aesthetic confusion. It was not possible to be serious about designing a motorcar as a carriage in 1930. Even for the King. It was not possible to design a baroque church in gothic style in 1719. It was not possible to design a university building as a Greek temple in 2000. It was not possible to design a Victorian village in 1995. It was not possible to design an airport building as a cottage in 1922. It was not possible to design a car as a 1930s replica in 1998, its engine deliberately decreased and more polluting. There would obviously be not a single thought about the people who would live in these places or use these objects. It is not possible to ignore light, sun, shadow, insulation or even heating systems. Does one prescribe historical clothing, cookers, and no bathrooms or electricity? Cut off telephone lines and ban TV aerials? This would lead to oppression. Dictatorships. Unfortunately there are still those who believe this nonsense is right in the third millennium.

1. Baroque church in gothic style. 2. Flying car. 3. Floating car. 4. Airport building, 1922. 5. Military bike. 6. Classical, 2000. 7. Stagecoach, 1885. 8. Classical, 1995. 9. Bus on rails, 1953. 10. Royal limousine, 1921.

97

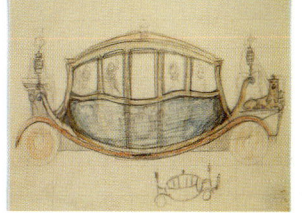

FOOD + DRINK

Why is food and drink such an underestimated element of the design process? It is an essential and crucial element. Maybe it is considered not intellectual enough by architects. Architects often pretend they are above all this. That extraordinary feeling, almost sensation, of having the first cup of coffee in the morning. That first sip of red wine in the evening. Or having a Martini-Rosso with a close friend. To have coffee and croissants on the terrace of the Café Flore in Paris. A drink in the Deux-Margot. To watch the skill of the waiters there – their aprons and shiny number discs. China and glasses as classic pieces of design developed over a few centuries. Definitely classic pieces here. Above all to sit and watch people go by. Mostly young ladies of course. Dinner for two in Brasserie Lipp in Paris must be top of my list of lifetime experiences. This is all too important to me. It is not a celebration of food and drink. To eat more. It is only to tell about the feelings I have. It is, and must be, part of the process of creating beautiful buildings. It is not just necessity but the art of eating. Eating and drinking can be more than an inspirational pleasure. Goulash and a pint of warm beer is certainly not.

The *plat du jour* was cassoulet. It made me hungry to read the name.'
E. Hemingway

1. Caprice restaurant, London. 2. Coffee. 3. Brandy. 4. Wine. 5. Modern food. 6. Deux Margot café, Paris. 7. Lunch. 8. Brasserie Lipp, Paris. 9. Horrible food.

1.
2.
3.
4.
5.
6.
7.
8.
9.

99

TOOLS

Revolution here was so fast that nobody remembers exactly when it began. Sometime in the mid-1980s the computer took over the design process. It will never be the same again. Every architectural or design office was suddenly full of computer screens. T-square, parallel motion, set square, scale, pins, tracing paper and Rotring pens became a piece of history practically overnight. At first this revolution did not help to produce better, more efficient, more beautiful and more human architecture. Not at all. For the first 10 years it was obvious that the results were actually more clumsy than those produced by hand. Only straight lines were possible. Programs were still too simple and operators not skilful enough. Even as late as 1990 it was impossible to find mechanical help to create the triangulated surface of the Future Systems Green building. It remains a hand product, and will remain so for a long time. There is seduction of a perfect line on the screen. Lines could be too abstract. The reality behind this is a new challenge. Process must remain by humans for humans. Can this process be fully computerised? Much, much later, if ever.

'Now that would be a challenge, to design a car as flexible as the horse.'
Peter Rice

1. Rotring pen. 2. Apple computer, 1998. 3. Calculator, 1973. 4. Historical tools. 5. Projector, 2002. 6. IBM Selectric-ball. 7. Computer hard drive, 2001. 8. Mouse, 2001.

1.
2.
3.
4.
5.
6.
7.
8.

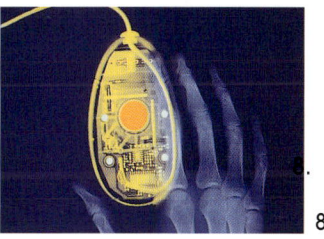

101

BRAIN + MACHINE

There is no contradiction or dilemma here. Both roles are easily defined. Conceptual work is done by the brain. It will be so for several more generations. Maybe forever. At this moment in time it is complete fantasy that machines can do basic concept. The brain is still used for basic data, identification of a problem, certain preconceptions, and even style. A conceptual sketch by hand identifies the basic idea. Even on a piece of scrap paper it is much quicker. Nothing much has changed since the time of Paxton, except that blotting paper is no longer produced. Full-size hand drawings are still used. Every new car begins life as a hand-drawn artist's impression. Even the Lunar module idea was conceived with the help of a hand sketch, and balsa-wood block and four pins model. On the other hand, the realisation of production drawings and pre-production models is totally the product of machines. The process of transfer into material reality is fully mechanised and robotic. Speed and precision is without precedent. Evolution of these programs is getting faster and faster. Production in materials is certainly not. There is some room for 'faster' new materials techniques here.

'Inventor is master.' E. Mendelsohn

1. Computer drawing. 2. Hand and pencil. 3. Sketch model. 4. I Sikorski, sketch. 5. Computer drawing. 6. Hand drawing. 7. I Issigonis, sketch. 8. Hand drawing.

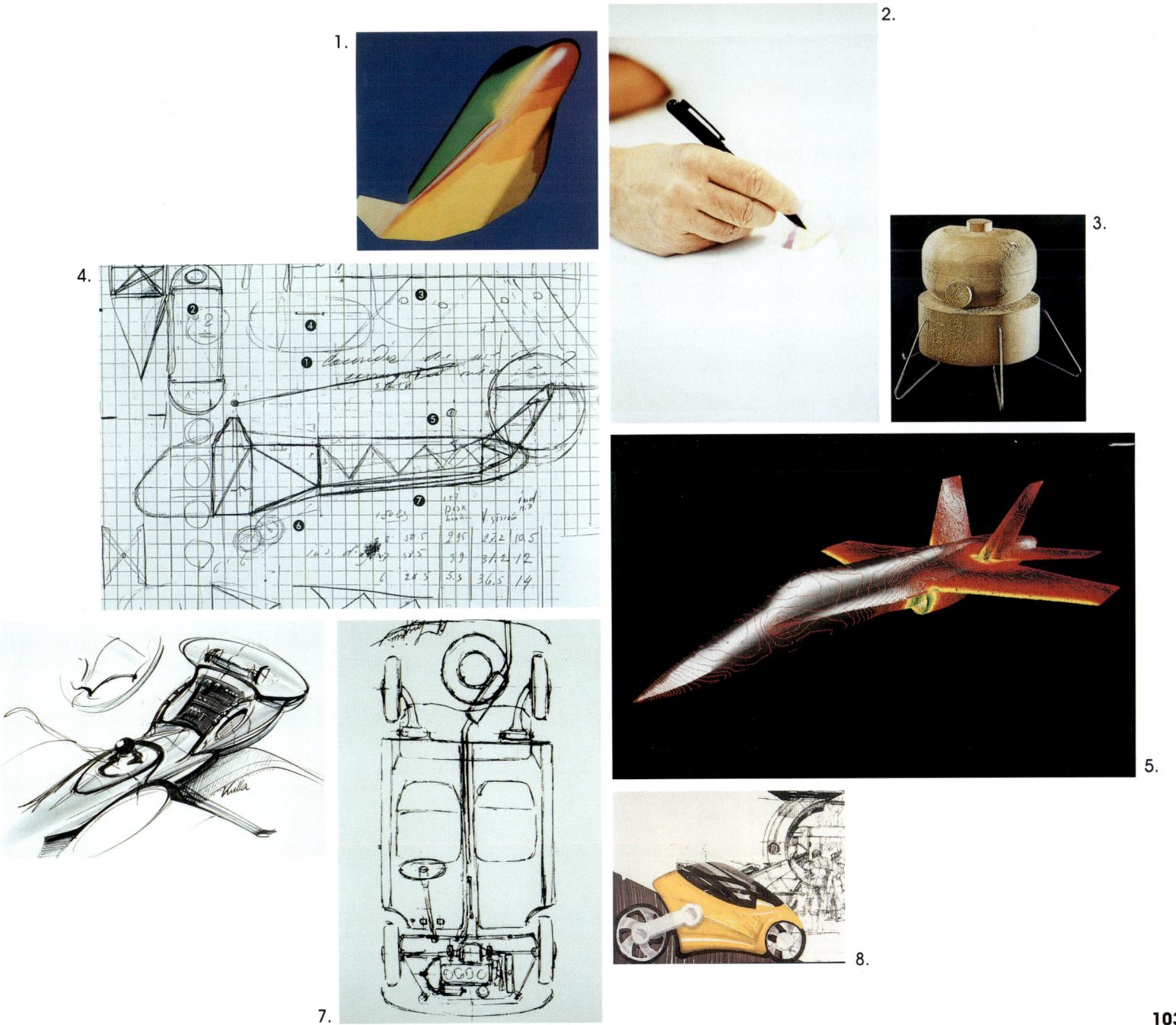

1.

2.

3.

4.

5.

6.

7.

8.

103

RESEARCH + TESTING

Research and testing are two words not often used in architecture. They are not common in this design world. Never used in architectural discussions. Hardly used in architectural magazines. Research building is a vehicle totally unknown in the building industry. Research of a school-building. Research of a house, or housing. Research of these types and others. Research of materials. Research of advance structures. Research of the past. Research of advanced forms of twentieth-century modern buildings, research of building form. Research of interior form. Research of everything. Research as a necessity to help the creative process. Testing is also an essential part of the creative process. In certain structures, particularly bridges, no testing could be fatal. Testing is a luxury in architecture and design. It is a legal requirement in car or aeroplane, and in the space industry. I can easily and confidently predict that research and testing will increase in architecture. More and more will be budgeted for this. More will be required from clients, more from legal bodies. All this will help architects in their search for new and more technically advanced and beautiful solution.

'Little by little the machine becomes part of humanity.' A. de Saint-Exupery

1. NASA test plane. 2. Clay mock-up. 3. Measurement module cap. 4. Frost testing. 5. Mock-up. 6. Bridge testing. 7. FS Selfridges mock-up, Birmingham, 2001. 8. Test vehicle. 9. Airbag test.

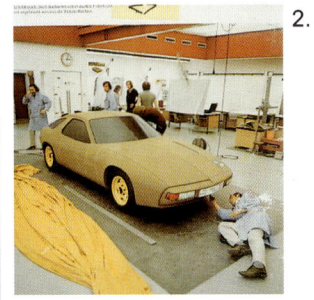

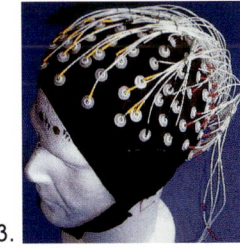

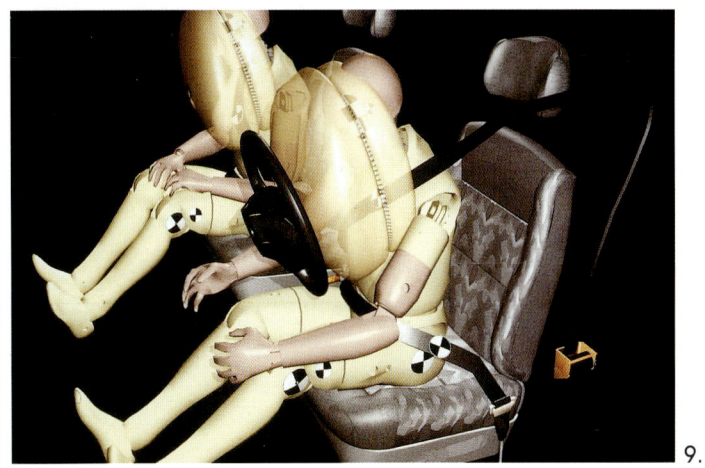

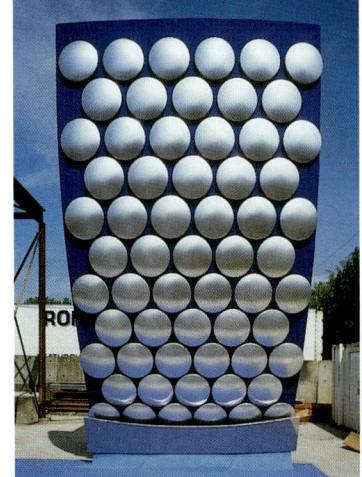

1.

2.

3.

4.

5.

6.

7.

8.

9.

105

1000 + 1 PEOPLE

Thousands and thousands of people are involved in the process of construction of one building, one intention, one object. From aluminium smelter, steel-mill worker, welder, carpenter, electrician. People digging bauxite ore in Baux, or those making paper on which to draw, to print. People making pencils, pens, rubbers, leads. People making carpets, glass, neoprene, silicon. People cutting, bending, laminating glass. Many architects consider this pool of knowledge, and human beings at least, in their work. Yet most of them do not. Many are completely ignorant of the manufacturing and building process. Totally unaware of the physical reality of these things being produced and constructed. Structural and mechanical engineers are another vital support. Again, another set of human beings. Yet often they are only just mentioned on the credit list. There are also hundreds of people that simply sit in meetings and create problems. I hope in the future it will not be the case just to 'produce' buildings, yes or no, and a money issue. We cannot only project-manage buildings, we must create and build them. We must protect the creative architectural process. By a thousand-and-one people, for people.

1. FS Meeting. 2. Site management. 3. Leadership. 4. Boatyard welders. 5. Manufacturing. 6. FS Model-making. 7. Team. 8. Factory work.

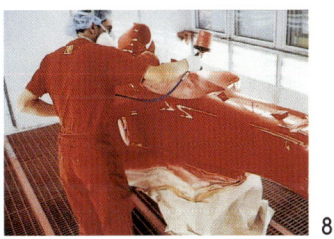

1.

2.

3.

4.

5.

6.

7.

8.

107

FS TEAM 1979–2002

SOREN AAGAARD   LINDY AITKIN   NERIDA BERGIN   SHEELAH BOOKATZ   LIDA CHARSOULI   SHEEMA CHAUHAN   JAKUB CIGLER   JONATHAN CLARK   FERNANDA CURI   TAMSYN CURLEY   HELENE DAHER   DESIREE DAVIS   SAM DONNELY   ADRIAN FOWLER   JULIAN FANNERY   HARVINDER GABHARI   KATY GHAVEMANI   DOMINIC HARRIS   NICOLA HAWKINS   ROSY HEAD   MATHEW HEYWOOD   SARAH JAYNE BOWEN   CANDAS JENNINGS   JAN KAPLICKY   NICOLA KIRKMAN   BILLY LEE   AMANDA LEVETE   IAIN MACKAY   NICHOLAS MANSOUR   ELIZABETH MIDDLETON   DAVID MILLER   GLENN MOORLEY   JEFF MORGAN   ANDREA MORGANTE   MARK NEWTON   DAVID NIXON   JOHN O'MARA   THORSTEIN OVERBERG   ANGUS POND   PETER RICHARDSON   REBECCA RICHWHITE   LIZ ROOT   JESSICA SALT   SEVERIN SODER   RACHEL STEVENSON   ANTONY ST LEGER

109

DIARY

It started a long time ago. Sometime in 1968. I was already in Britain. I had a great need to make a record of my everyday thoughts. To draw everyday thinking. At first the drawings were very small and simple. One did not know how. The number of entries were very limited. Sometimes one per month. But often even more time passed before another entry appeared. There was even the problem of the right notebook. To find the right paper. Above all the right type of pen. In those days the choice of pen was very limited. Lines were of course black. Colour came much later. Colour pencils and pens. Almost from the first day I began to use cut-outs from magazines. Pictures of details, whole objects, people, buildings. Ugly things as well. Diagrams. Headlines. Quotations. Sometimes even a postage stamp of the day. The diaries are quite private but an essential tool of the design process. Now the entries are a few pages every day, and I have a pocket version for when I am travelling. I often like to look back on what I was thinking a few years ago. It is almost like reading a bible. Sometimes even the weather is recorded.

'An artist is above all responsible towards himself.' M. Davis

1. Diary page, 1990. 2. Diary cover, 1994. 3. Diary cover, 1969. 4. Pocket diary. 5. Diaries. 6. Diary, 1988. 7. Diary page, 2001. 8. Diary cover, 1997.

1. 10-12-90 lundi
A+J residence

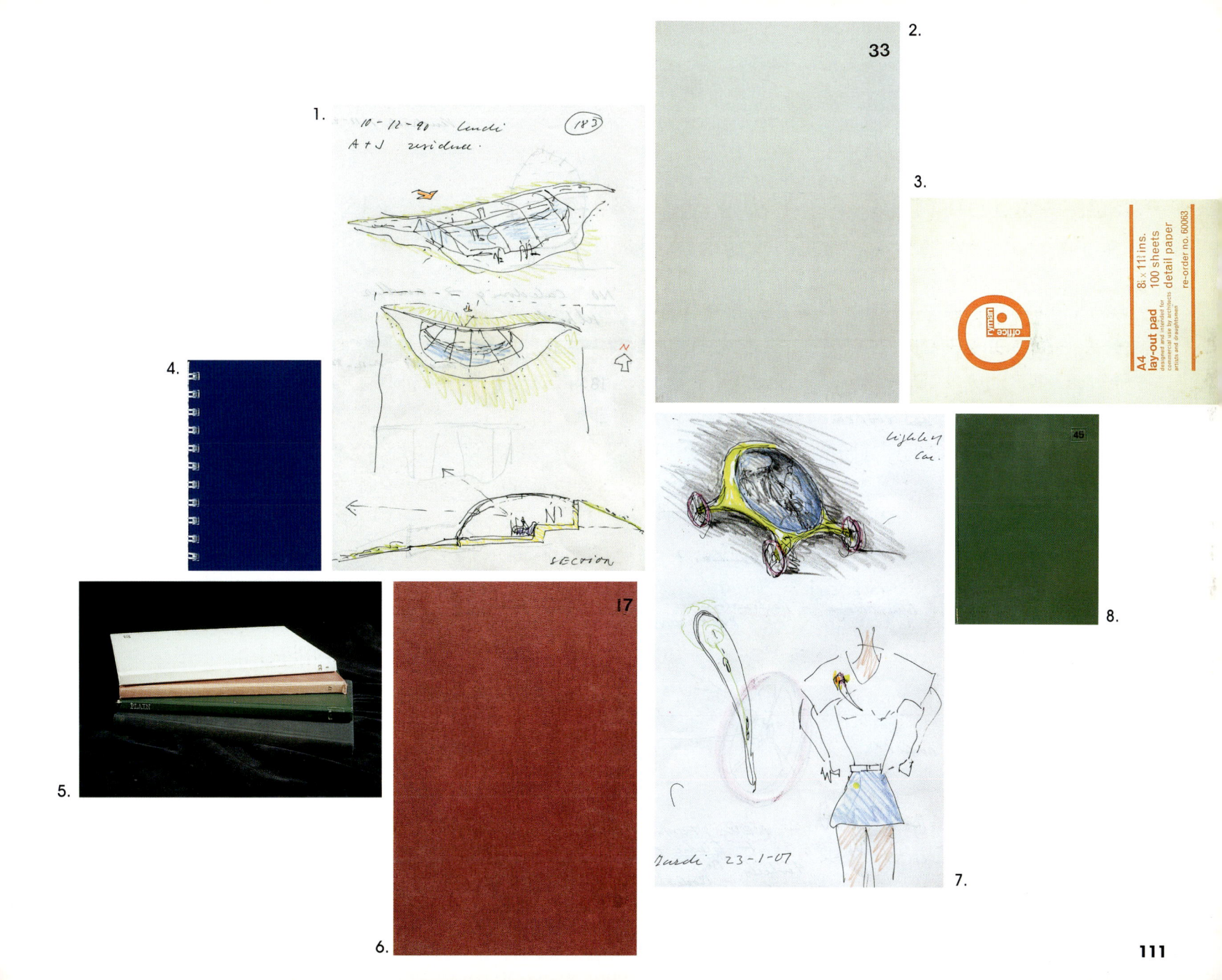

183

SECTION

2. 33

3. 8½ x 11¾ ins.
100 sheets
detail paper
re-order no. 60063

ryman office
A4 lay-out pad
designed and intended for
commercial use by architects
artists and draughtsmen

4.

5.

6. 17

7. lightly car.

Bardi 23-1-07

8. 45

111

SKETCH

Even a very long time ago I had a desire to draw. From humble beginnings at architectural school, or perhaps just after. One of the first architectural drawings was of course a classical Greek column head. Even the equipment was ancient. No ballpoint pen. Only a pencil or ordinary pen and a bottle of ink. A stick of charcoal. The fear of an empty sheet of paper is still sometimes with me. The fear of what others would say. To show sketches to your teachers was almost painful. Probably my real break came when one sketch was reproduced in a magazine. Suddenly there was no more privacy of conceptual sketch. Only a few architects expose their true early sketches. It is not considered commercially acceptable. But I do. To have a pile of clean white paper in front of me and to do some sketches gives me enormous pleasure. In the office, home, on the train or even flying 10,000 metres above the ground. That little piece of paper, shaky hand and simple or clumsy lines should have everything. Shape, size, colour, materials and structure. When the concept sketch is right the whole concept is right. It is the right beginning. Machines cannot replace this. Not yet. It is highly emotional. Process and product. Sometimes I sweat.

'In architecture it is possible to explain design with a small sketch.'   O. Niemeyer

1. JK Tree, 1967. 2. JK Bikini, 1990. 3. FS Champagne bucket, 1991. 4. FS Bibliotheque National, Paris. 1989. 5. FS Media Centre, London, 1996. 6. FS Selfridges building, Birmingham, 1999. 7. FS Green Bird, London, 1996. 8. FS Hauer/King House, London, 1992.

1.

2.

3.

4.

5.

6.

7.

8.

113

DRAWING

I remember endless evenings – Saturdays, Sundays, Christmas days – just drawing. Often with some jazz music in the background and of course a cup of coffee. Many of them. They were, they are, wonderful moments. A very peaceful time. Patience and tranquillity. Little battles with paper or film. Every line thickness in careful balance. It was a relatively primitive process, the inspiration coming from car or aeroplane presentations. A collection of stencils helped the process. Quite a high number. Stencils from many countries and many professions. Sets of French curves that allowed the drawing of truly curvy objects. Curvy buildings. Very unusual in those days. Simply adding curvy lines together is art on its own. I used curvy lines more and more, and the T-square started to disappear. I started with a ruling pen and a bottle of ink. Then a rather primitive Rotring pen. Then finally a set of pens to draw on film, and cartridges of special ink. I still have a set. I have a sad feeling that I no longer draw in this way. Machines certainly took over. I still do some critical ones using this process. Sometimes.

1. JK Cliff cabin, 1967. 2. JK House for a helicopter pilot, 1979. 3. FS Car, 2001. 4. FS House in Wales, 1994. 5. FS Twentyfirst-century gallery, London, 1993. 6. FS Green Building, London, 1990. 7. FS Concrete house, Prague, 1960.

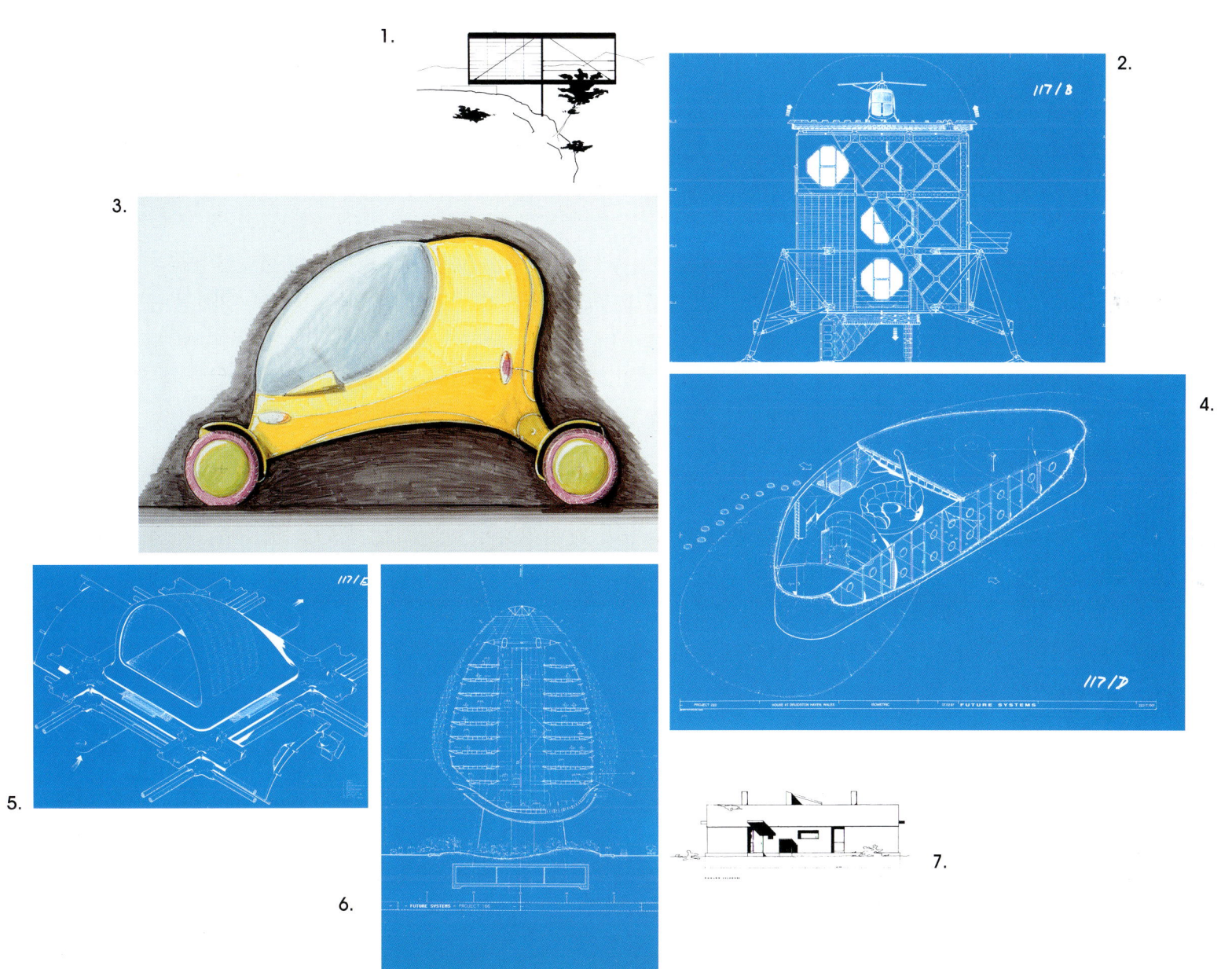

1.

2.

3.

4.

5.

6.

7.

115

PHOTOMONTAGE

The question was how to represent new thinking in a new way. How to show new types of buildings that somebody would like and understand. Maybe even the desire to shock a little bit. A new way of how to rediscover my shuttered identity. How to find new form. How to be artistic. How to introduce new reality. How to introduce the realism of the site. Photomontage is a relatively fast technique. Certainly a technique introduced many decades ago. It is also an attempt to relate architecture to other art disciplines. It was definitely different from the kitschy watercolour perspectives of the day. Of course this was a long time before it was possible to use the computer for such processes. It was a personal product. I still resent the anonymity of computer drawing. It still has little unique feeling. Computer images can promote bad architecture. The difference between good or bad is almost zero. But the unique personal touch is returning. We are almost there with Future Systems' unique computer-generated photomontage. It is after all the year 2002. The third millennium.

1. JK Photomontage, 1975. 2. FS Selfridges building, Birmingham, 1999. 3. JK Photomontage, 1994. 4. JK House for a helicopter pilot, 1978. 5. JK Photomontage, 1978. 6. JK Photomontage 1976.

1.

2.

3.

4.

5.

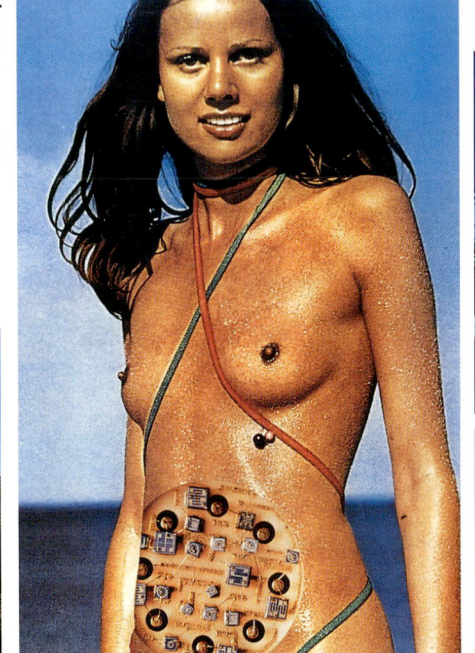

6.

117

MODEL + MOCK-UP

These are vital tools for me. Visualisation is impossible without them. Clients like them. Architects like them. The practicality of a proposal is easily established, form can be tested. The use of colour can be tested. Creating final form without a model is impossible, particularly in a world of plastic architecture. Even the use of a simple, tiny plasticine model can be used to establish the principal shape and to start to think in the right scale. For example a major decision on the back window of Future Systems' Media Centre was made by cutting off a plasticine model in the right place. Cutting blocks of polystyrene. Filing down the final form can be extremely exciting. Suddenly the final form is here. At Future Systems we all do it. There is pleasure in helping to create presentation models. The model arrives in the office. A crowd of people gather round. Suddenly it is all fixed. Changes are possible only through drawings. Mock-up in architecture is still relatively rare. To see the components working together in reality for the first time is breathtaking luxury. Other design fields use mock-up all the time. Architects can learn something from this. Even building model aeroplane kits give me much pleasure. The richness of their form is staggering. I still make them. Many.

1. FS Zero Emission Development (ZED), London, 1995. 2. FS Paris Museum, 1999. 3. Model aeroplane. 4. FS Caravan, 1991. 5. FS Chaise longue, 1986. 6. FS Fauteuil, 1998. 7. FS Construction tower, 1997. 8. FS NASA table, 1988.

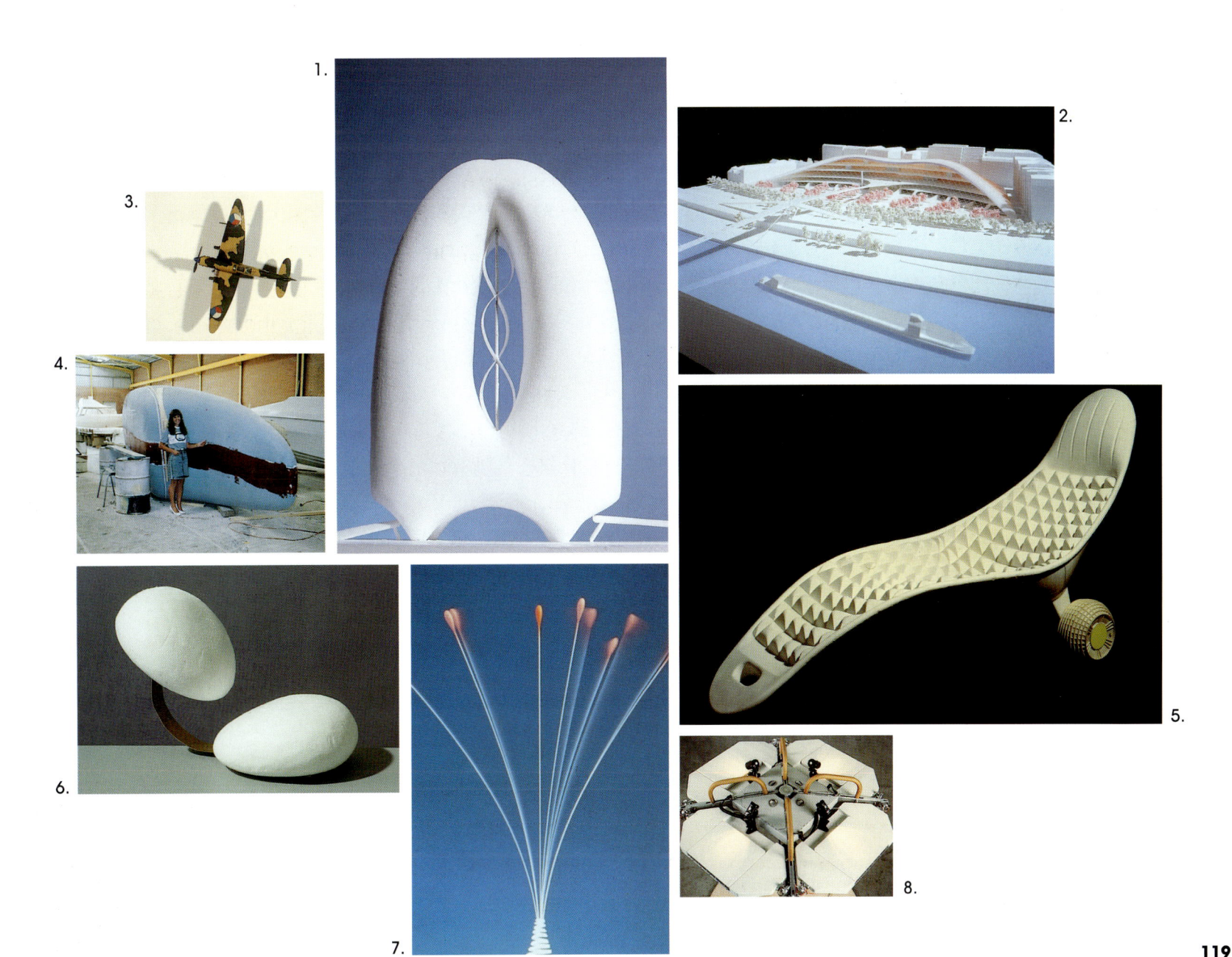

1.

2.

3.

4.

5.

6.

7.

8.

119

DESIGN

Is so-called design different from architecture? Of course not. I cannot see any difference at all. For me design is simply small elements of architecture. From tiny objects to large exhibitions. To design a small flower-pin is a real pleasure – the shape, practicalities of pinning it on the dress, the flower arrangement, bending of the steel plate and size and weight. Also the design of hangers for the Marni shop as practical and beautiful affordable objects – an integral part of the shop. The creation of mini textile objects to sunbathe or swim. Every square millimetre matters. Elegance is priority. The ultimate product is of course in the hands of a skilful seamstress. An aluminium and stainless steel table for eight people – only 40 kilos. No calculations, no testing – one has to rely entirely on experience. A plywood table or freestanding cupboard for two. Future Systems' exhibitions require a very personal touch – the budget is minimal – and a striking effect. A pollution-free bus, probably a generation ahead of any other bus design, with an advanced semi-monocoque body-design for increased capacity. Bodywork free of wheels. Four-wheel steering. Of course nobody is interested – the year was 1993.

'Lack of daring innovation.' R. Loewy

1. FS Faggianato Gallery Exhibition, 2001. 2. JK Bikini, 1988. 3. FS Aluminium table, 1997. 4. FS Marni hanger, 1999. 5. FS Superbus, 1993. 6. FS Vogue table, 1999. 7. FS Dinghy, 1996. 8. FS Flowerpin, 2001. 9. FS Wooden table, 1998.

1.

2.

3.

4.

5.

6.

7.

8.

9.

121

ARCHITECTURE

My history here is a long one. It is more than 40 years since I built my first project. Of course I was alone. There was not much help from anybody. I was still at school at the age of 21. My first interior job completed. My first Le Corbusier book open. Discouraged by my professor. The project was a flat in sixteenth-century roof space. Roof trusses painted with bulls blood against rot. Painted with pink whitewash fire-proof paint in the Second World War. My friend did the plastering, another welded the tubular furniture. There were few paintings on the wall. However this was a roof terrace with fabulous views of Prague castle. Then there was the exhibition of my father's work. In the middle of my two years of national service. Then my first real job. Garden, terrace, mini-golf rails, ramp and house interior. My first serious steel structure and first use of a structural engineer – my friend of course. Then Kafka's Memorial in collaboration with its sculptor. A little family house with a studio under construction when the Russian tanks arrived. Then my quick departure to England. After this I did not have an opportunity to build for five years. Conversion of my own flat was the first project. Then the Brighton Marina involvement. And then we won a competition for a factory unit with D. Nixon. Of course they did not build it. In the meantime, every evening, Saturday and Sunday, more drawing and photomontages. Future Systems was invented.

'I believe in emotional architecture'. L. Barragan

1. JK House and garden, Prague, 1965. 2. JK Attic flat, Prague, 1958. 3. JK Brighton Marina, 1976. 4. JK Kafka Memorial, Prague, 1965. 5. JK FD house and studio, 1967. 6. FS Factory, 1976. 7. JK Archery Steps, London, 1974. 8. JK Josef Kaplicky's Exhibition, Prague, 1964. 9. FS Industrial Nursery Mk2, 1985.

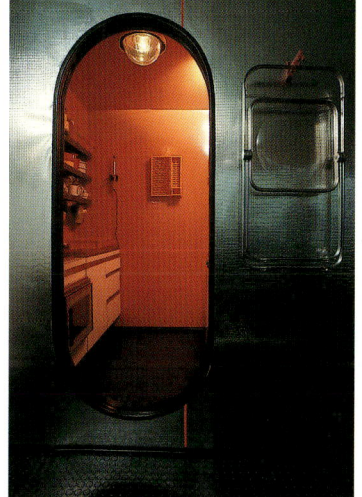

1.

2.

3.

4.

5.

6.

7.

8.

9.

ARCHITECTURE

Once the name of Future Systems was officially registered, there was no work. Of course. Postmodernism was reaching its peak. Prince Charles was on full attack. Then a famous competition for a number of grand buildings on Trafalgar Square in London was announced. We designed a quite revolutionary office building. Form, structure, eco systems, solar collector. This was 1985, and the design was only laughed at. Too much ahead of its time. After 15 years it is now a respected design. Even copied. A later competition was for the Bibliotheque National in Paris. Fifteen leading architects from around the world were invited. Again we produced a totally new form. Open to the people. Suspended glazing. A pedestrian bridge through the building. Expandable storage. What a surprise – we came second. The office consisted of three people. Next was a beautiful building designed to house the collection of Acropolis marbles in Athens. Again, completely revolutionary thinking. No-architecture architecture. The structure no higher than the trees around it. A solar shield on the south side. A demountable tent for the British Film Institute. The first true buildings for Future Systems. Then came two private houses. An urban site in London. A house on a beautiful seaside site in Wales, complimentary to the site and seashore nearby. Glass and grass. Suddenly one was not only designing but also building. After all those years.

'Real architecture does not need words.' C. Ellwood

1. FS Coexistence, 1984. 2. FS MoMi Tent, London, 1991. 3. FS Museum, Athens, 1990. 4. FS Bibliotheque National, 1989. 5. FS Deployable truss Mk2, 1985. 6. FS Blob, London. 7. FS Hauer/King House, London, 1992. 8. FS Spire, 1988. 9. FS House in Wales, 1994.

1.

2.

3.

4.

5.

6.

7.

8.

9.

125

ARCHITECTURE

In 1995 came another extraordinary opportunity. We won a limited competition for a Media centre at Lord's Cricket Ground in London. This was a real, real challenge. From the first sketch it was conceived as an all-aluminium semi-monocoque structure to be made at a boatyard. This had never been done before. Fire-proofing of aluminium had also never been done before. It included a 40 metres wide glass wall through which the game could be seen. We achieved not just this, but also the complete satisfaction of two hundred journalists and reporters. It had a monochrome light-blue interior with soft acoustic lining. New architecture, a structural and building form. Like a camera overlooking the grounds. A clear indication of future building forms. Journalists called it a garden shed. But of course. In the meantime we began work on several Comme des Garcons shops. First was an aluminium entrance tunnel for the New York shop, made in England then shipped to the US. Then a 50 metres long double-curved and fritted glass wall for the Tokyo shop. Both represented a totally new vision for a fashion shop. We delivered a new image for Comme des Garcon shops. Many years ahead of competition. Then there was the research project for Green Bird – proof of the possibility of a tall green building. Very advanced eco-systems. The study for the Josef K. House – I am sure it will be built one day. New forms researched and tested all the time.

1. FS Green Bird, London, 1996. 2. FS Josef K. House, 1997. 3. FS Marni, London, 1999. 4. FS Comme des Garcons, New York, 1998. 5. FS Media Centre, London, 1995. 6. FS Zero Emission Development (ZED), Berlin, 1995. 7. FS Docklands Bridge, 1996. 8. FS Comme des Garcons, Tokyo, 1998

1.

2.

3.

4.

5.

6.

7.

8.

127

ARCHITECTURE

The Media Centre at Lord's Cricket Ground finally opened in 1999 to the great applause of its users. After that there was nothing. Nothing to do. 'Blind' newspaper journalists described the building as a 'blob', garden shed, space station. Then came a breakthrough. Selfridges. A brand new department store 25,000 square metres in Birmingham, England. A visionary client, open brief, and endless possibilities. We designed the backdrop for the Victorian church next to it. A complete contrast to the rest of the development in primitive American postmodern style. A roof garden, terraces, a bridge, atrium, colours, sculptural form, people everywhere. The whole external surface covered with 30,000 aluminium discs. Lighting and an image with no need for a big sign on the main door. More challenges were to follow. There were the Marni shops in London, Milan, Paris and New York. A large motor-show stand for Ferrari cars in Frankfurt where we tried to match the beauty of the cars with architecture of dynamic display. A memorial in Prague completely rejected by a jury full of old friends – never again would we try there. Also three experimental classrooms in London. A travelling demountable pavilion for Vodka. And above all, the South Bank competition entry with sculptor Anish Kapoor. The Natural History Museum Extension. Certainly an indication of things to come. Maybe even more. The future is here.

'Not the hard inflexible straight line created by man.'   O. Niemeyer

1. FS World classrooms, London, 2001. 2. FS Marni, Milan, 2001. 3. FS Ferrari stand, Frankfurt, 2001. 4. FS and A. Kapoor, South Bank, London, 2001. 5. FS Selfridges building, Birmingham, 1999. 6. FS Selfridges foodhall, Manchester, 2001. 7. FS Memorial, Prague, 2000. 8. FS Vodka Pavilion, New York, 2001.

1.

2.

3.

4.

5.

6.

7.

8.

129

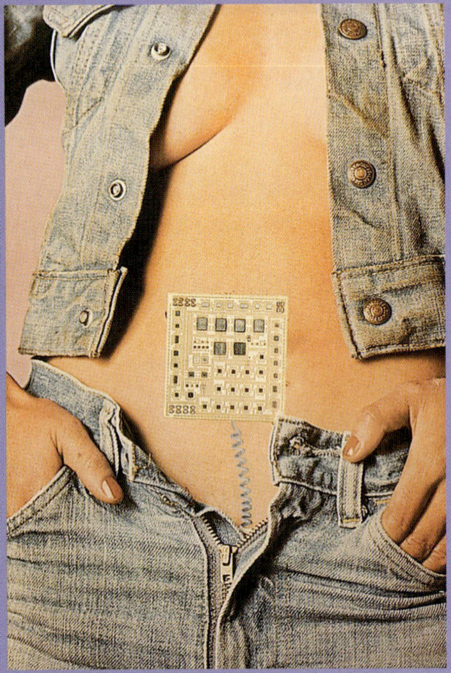

LIFE

LIFE

It all started a long, long time ago. For me, major historical events in Europe were part of my life. I cannot and I will not forget such events. Politics were not only for politicians but also part of life – my life. The destiny of millions of people. These events were not something happening somewhere to someone else, but something happening to me. Until I came to England, I had lived most of my life in dictatorships – fascist and communist. The influence of all of this on my thinking generally, architecturally, was enormous. My preconceptions were endless. My judgement of people was also influenced. This probably had its advantages. Life is not just fun, but a serious time. However there were many disadvantages – architecturally, self-education, self searching for the facts, coming from a country we know nothing about and where one's mother tongue is not English. It is an amazing privilege to now live in London, one of the main centres of architectural thinking in the world. In Europe. Being around architectural revolutions like Archigram, the Pompidou Centre, Willis Faber's Dumas Building and many others. Just to be allowed to live and work in a free country is a privilege. I will never forget that.

'Fascism and communism was life and death, not just politics.' JK

1. Prague, 1937. 2. Prague, 1968. 3. Communist poster, 1952. 4. Nazi poster, 1938. 5. Millennium Dome, 1999. 6. Willis Faber building, Ipswich, 1973. 7. Prague, 1989. 8. Prague, 1945.

133

IN MY LIFETIME

What happened to relatively simple products? The telephone is an astonishing example. In such a short time there has been a complete change. A completely new culture. The telephone was once a black box somewhere in the hall. One had to stand to use it. I was of course not allowed to use it as a child. And it could only be used for local calls. Only 20 years ago it was difficult to make calls to other countries. And in this time, this is still not automatic in many countries. Calls to the US even as recently as the mid-1980s had a disturbing echo voice in the background. Before the introduction of satellites calls were very expensive indeed. So does all this help human relationships? The answer is certainly yes. Young people completely rely on it. Even powerful politicians have 'hot-lines' between two countries. Several international crisises have been avoided this way. No more Pearl Harbors. But this progress cannot replace personal contact. How many people do we now know as voice only? One cannot see the colour of their hair or eyes, and can only guess their character. The mobile phone is here, video phone is on its way. A phone where we can talk in different languages is possible. All this in my lifetime. What will come next?

1. Telephone, 1937. 2. Mobile phone, 2001. 3. Military phone, 1940. 4. Bell 1 Model 300, 1937. 5. Visual phone. 6. Mobile phone in use. 7. Mobile phone in use. 8. Siemens phone, 1966.

1.

2.

3.

4.

5.

6.

7.

8.

135

IN MY LIFETIME

Even more astonishing than evolution in design and stagnation in architecture is what has happened at the beaches of St. Tropez, Copacabana, Malibu or Florida. A complete revolution in what we wear. From the almost complete cover of sixty years ago to more-or-less nothing. These sophisticated items are not the products of fashion designers but people themselves. They never feature in *Vogue*. It is not without interest that the bikini revolution was started by an engineer. One can still see the first pattern drawing. The pattern needed to work technically. The choice of fabric and perfect use of material properties. Later the use of new materials. The engineering is unique in that it must fit the curves. The best are probably made at home, and sold on beaches. Sometimes there is a battle of the square millimetres – a total visual effect. Simple beauty. It almost cannot be ugly. The body is the main actor. Then one half is abandoned. More than thirty years ago, even more skill was put into one little triangle of fabric. With jeans, trench coat and trainers, the bikini is one of the classics of modern living. What an inspiration.

1. France, 1937. 2. Brazil, 1996. 3. Czechoslovakia, 1937. 4. France, 2001. 5. Brazil, 1995. 6. Beach, 2002. 7. France, 1946. 8. France, 1945. 9. Brazil, 1998.

137

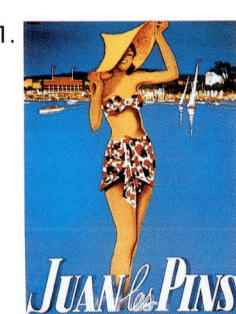

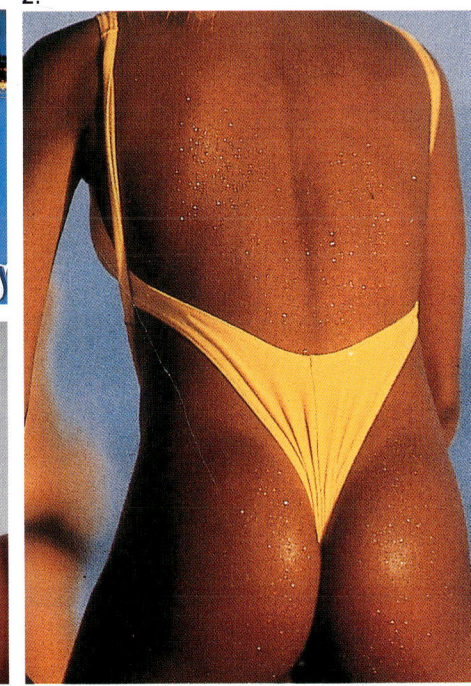

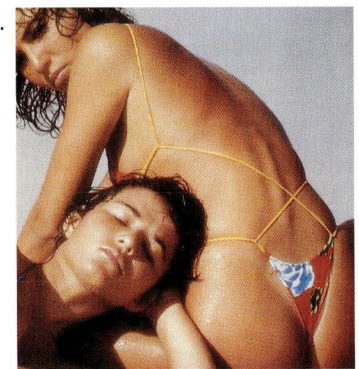

IN MY LIFETIME

There have been extraordinary developments in almost every other area except architecture. The house model of 1937 has not been surpassed by the 2001 model. Architecture is the only profession in the world that quite often is moving backwards. This is an almost perverse trend. It is a complete mystery to me. Look at art, music, fashion, films – fundamental changes are occurring. Experiments, new thinking, new designs are quite evident. Only architecture is influenced by those who hold on to the past. Or is this backwardness implemented by designers who do not know any better? Kitsch and horrible houses are in great demand by people with money. Others follow. Have you ever seen a beautiful modern house in Hollywood? Never. In the end the architects have also to answer many questions. Many of them never create anything forward-looking, or even think about it. More creativity is required. More books to look at, and even more creativity… Every other profession is looking forward. Why not architecture?

1. P. Johnson, 1949. 2. N. Foster, 1973. 3. P. R. Williams, 1961. 4. Adoul, Hartwig and Gerodias, 1937. 5. J. Nouvel, 2001. 6. Pop star's house, 1995. 7. G. Baas and L. Stokla, 1938. 8. House, 2000.

1.
2.
3.
4.
5.
6.
7.
8.

139

1937

CAROLINA AIVARS   PETER BELL   MADDY BENNET   SEAN BILLINGS   PAVE
CIGLER   VACLAV CIGLER   JIRI CIZEK   BRIAN CLARKE   JANA CLAVERIE SARA
DVORAK   DENISA DVORAKOVA   DICK ERNEST   GERARD FAGGIONAT
DONNA HARRIS   KATY HARRIS   DEBRA HAUER   RON HERRON   RICHAR
MICHAELA KADNEROVA   JIRINA KAPLICKA   JOSEF KAPLICKY   JOSE
KOLAR   VLADIMIR KUCERA   AMANDA LEVETE   IVAN MARGOLIUS   JARMIL
NEWBY   DAVID NIXON   MARTIN PAWLEY   FRANCK PEACOCK   A. AND
CERVIN ROBINSON   RICHARD ROGERS   TANIA RUDISHULI   DORIS SAATCH
ADRIENA SIMOTOVA   WILF STEVENSON   VLADIMIR SUCHANEK   DEYA
MATTHEW WALLES   JONATHAN WAXMAN   HANK WIEKENS

OBEK   KLAUS BODE   JOANN BRANTHWAITE   JOSEPH BRUMLIK   JAKUB
OLLIER   PETER COOK   RICHARD DAVIES   JAROSLAV DIETL   EMMANUEL
ARCUS FIELD   NORMAN FOSTER   DAVID GLOVER   JONATHAN HARPER
ORDEN   MILAN HROMADKA   TONY HUNT   EVA JIRICNA   JIRI JOHN
APLICKY JNR   A. AND S. KAPOOR   JARMILA KARAS   JEREMY KING   JIRI
ARKOVA   G. AND B. MARSHALL-ANDREWS   ANNE MINOGUE   FRANK
OPPY   TONY PRITCHARD   VITTORIO RADICE   JOHN RANDLE   PETER RICE
USANE SCHNOBLINGOVA   ANDY SEDGWICK   DON SHUTTLEWORTH
DJIC   NICKI TIBBLES   JANA TICHA   MAJA VARADJAN   LJUBA VESELY

2002

JOSEF KAPLICKY

Josef Kaplicky was my father. I owe him quite a lot. He gently introduced me to architecture, culture, art, everything. He was a sculptor, painter, graphic designer, writer and architect himself. He tried very hard to teach me. He showed me books. He introduced me to the big names in architecture, such as Adolf Loos. A book on Le Corbusier suddenly appeared on my desk. My father was a true inspiration. The Germans came, war came, communists took over. All these events slowly destroyed him. He was not allowed to exhibit, he was not allowed to teach. He became ill. It was a tragic end. It was devastating for me to witness this destruction of a gentle human being. He died early. He left his sculptures, drawings and writings. These are an enormous support and inspiration to me. A few years ago they were all withdrawn from the collection in the National Gallery in Prague. The final act of this tragedy. He was a freedom-loving man. I miss him a lot.

Josef Kaplicky 1899–1962

'Good architecture will always be that which is not some cultural occasion for a few but a total part of street and life.' Josef Kaplicky

1. Torso, 1934. 2. Book cover, 1933. 3. Own garden, 1935. 4. Sketch, 1933. 5. Josef Kaplicky. 6. Torso, 1932. 7. Stained glass, 1931. 8. Stamp, 1947. 9. Poster, 1936.

143

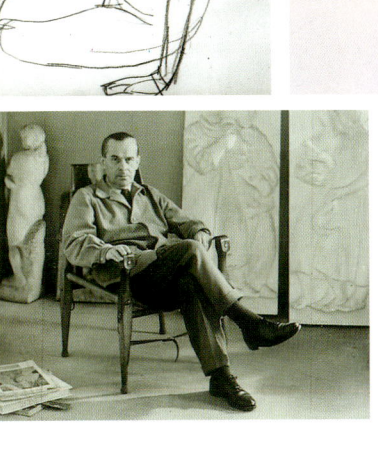

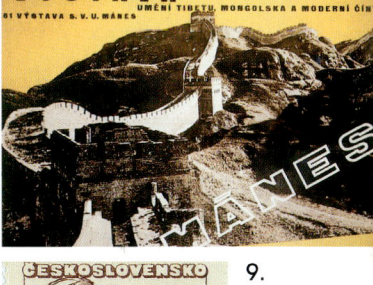

JIRINA KAPLICKA

Jirina Kaplicka was my mother. An outstanding person. Totally devoted to her flower drawings. Devoted to her friends. To my father. To me. Devoted to life. It was not easy – two world wars, 6 years of fascism and 40 years of communism. She was supportive of my father all his life, through good times and bad times. She was amazingly strong. A symbol of strength for the much younger people around her. People respected her. One day when I was already in England a postcard came. On the front side was a Greek windmill, on the flip side only one word – 'Future'. It took my breath away. She was right. This is the future of mankind. We had ritual telephone conversation every Sunday morning. It was like going to church. I think of her quite a lot. I miss her very much. Sometimes I would like to ask her advice. Only hundreds and hundreds of flower drawings and many books survive. I use her drawings as inspiration for my projects.

Jirina Kaplicka 1901–1984

'A poppy seed is tiny, but what strength is held inside.'   Jirina Kaplicka

1. Watercolour, 1976. 2. Jirina Kaplicka. 3. Plant book, 1976. 4. Plant book, 1986. 5. Studio, 1975. 6. J. Kotera, Jirina Kaplicka,1919. 7. Windmill postcard, 1974. 8. Watercolour, 1970

1.

2.

3.

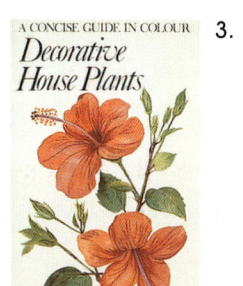

4. Jiřina Kaplická
Kytice
Kytky
Kytičky

5.

6.

7.

8.

145

1937–1940

It all started a long time ago in the city of Prague. There was still peace around in Europe. No German occupation yet. It is nice to think about my childhood. Only my favourite toys to play with. No worries, no school. I still remember some of my toys. A Greyhound bus, a white streamline caravan with rubber wheels. A little train. It all meant quite a lot. No toys were available in the shops. Later every toy came from older children. Every toy was treasured. Were these first architectural feelings too? Yes, probably. No tea, no coffee. No oranges – only for German children. A pair of shoes inherited from neighbours. Later wooden soles on your shoes. Coupons. Artificial honey. Little gas masks issued. The first visit to the cinema. This was all happening in Prague. Modern architecture everywhere. Adolf Loos's Muller House only 100 metres away. The sugar-white house one could see from our window. An occasional visit there. But my love for beautiful things certainly started here. I lived in a modern interior and garden, designed by my father. That experience will stay with me forever. The strong architectural influences were already present. Even that early.

1. House where JK was born, Prague. 2. Prague, 1937. 3. Nativity figure. 4. Stamp. 5. Children's book. 6. Greyhound bus toy. 7. A. Loos Muller House, Prague. 8. Poster, 1937. 9. Prague tram. 10. Banknote.

147

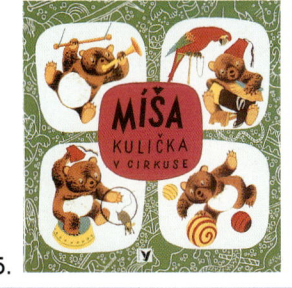

1940–1943

Prague where I was born was a modern city. It had more modern architecture per head than any other European city. It was everywhere. Shops, schools, cinemas, Tatra cars, trams, even park benches. Colony Baba was all modern houses. We went there for Sunday walks. Friends lived in modern houses. All this must have had a fundamental impact on me. Modern was almost the norm. I remember a lecture on Rodin. I remember the Burghers of Calais sculpture. I was about five. My first lessons in English, many of them in an air-raid shelter. Father drew me a 'Normandie' liner on the bedroom wall. An enormous one. Of course with me looking out from the cabin window. This prompted my first desire to travel. In the meantime, occupation and war was going on around me. Listening to the BBC every night. That was punishable by death. The 'Churchill' plug-in device was inserted instead of short waves, removed by Germans. The sound of Beethoven's Ninth drums. I was going to sleep. 'Ici Londres' I said clearly in a tram. My mother went white. You could be shot for that.

1. Toy soldier. 2. Prague, 1941. 3. *Signal* magazine. 4. A. Rodin, 'The Burghers of Calais'. 5. Stamp. 6. Schuco toy car. 7. 'Normandie' liner. 8. Concentration camp. 9. Frdebel bricks toy.

149

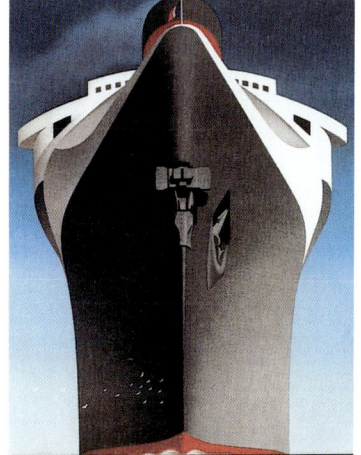

1943–1945

War was getting closer. You could not escape it. Even children could not avoid it. A few artists came every Sunday evening. Then the first serious air-raids. And then you could see them for the first time. Silver aeroplanes with long tails of white vapour. Anti-radar silver foils falling down. Fascinated of course by British and American planes. They were different, more rounded. The first pictures of the Spitfire, Flying Fortress, Mosquito in a German book. We played pilots. Rations were getting smaller and smaller. Milk was only for children. No chocolate. Beetroot marmalade. The first American truck still in German hands. It was different, more round and painted olive green. We just whispered around. Then one morning came revolution. I went through the streets with the Czech flag. They could shoot me for that. Revolution started. German jets bombed Prague. The Vlasov army in German uniforms tried to save Prague. And they did. Our house was under sniper fire. Then they came. The first tank. The Russians. We shook their hands. They smiled back. We did not realise another occupation had just begun. This time for 44 years.

1. Compulsory radio display. 2. D-Day, 1944. 3. Kriegsflugzeuge book. 4. JK Sketch, 1944. 5. Air-raid. 6. Prague, 1945. 7. Prague, 1945. 8. US truck.

1. Pamatuj, Pamatuj,

že poslouchání zahraničního rozhlasu je zakázáno a trestá se káznicí nebo i smrtí.

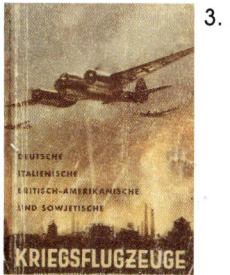

3. KRIEGSFLUGZEUGE

1945–1948

The Russians came as 'liberators' in 1945. Freedom? Thousands of German prisoners marched through the streets. Then two-and-a-half years of relative freedom. One could feel it. Magazines and books coming, people visiting. The US military band in silver helmets. A silver B-17 on the ground. The first copy of *Life* magazine. The first famous khaki cans from UNRRA. The first chewing gum in a yellow wrapper. The first white T-shirt from the US. The first American car. New spirit. New hopes. We were naive. Things were already decided in Yalta. Nobody around knew. The existence of the Iron Curtain was proclaimed by Churchill. The Curtain was certainly rolling down. It finally rolled down with the communist putsch in 1948. I remember that day exactly. There was snow and it was cold. I did not truly understand but I knew something very bad was happening. Another form of occupation began. We started to listen to the BBC, Voice of America, once again. People were disappearing, escaping abroad, being arrested. There were endless rumours. Concentration camps, prisons, terror, particularly in the first years, until Stalin's death. In Czechoslovakia at one time there were 250,000 people in various prisons and camps.

1. Iron Curtain, 1948. 2. *Life*, 1945. 3. J. Zrzavy painting. 4. Stamp. 5. B-17 bomber. 6. Czech armour, Prague, 1945. 7. US car. 8. Elementary school entrance. 9. Stamp. 10. Chewing gum.

153

1948–1951

During this period there was an extraordinary contrast around. On the surface everything was normal. Complete control of one party. Dictatorship. Culture ceased to exist. Architecture ceased to exist. Literature ceased to exist. Socialist realism was introduced into art and architecture as the only possibility. In the meantime my family and I tried to survive. Mentally. Physically. Old friends became communists. Small circles of friends would visit my parents and me. I constructed my first model aeroplane. It flew. It was not a kit, but had to be made from pieces of wood and paper. No balsa wood. Primitive glue. I had my first lessons in using tools, cutting, gluing. It was a new world. The beginning of a great love affair with aeroplanes and ships. It was certainly architecture. I am still in love with that world. Every Saturday and Sunday, cutting and gluing. Holidays in the lake country. The execution of my first drawings for a yacht model. It sailed beautifully. My parents bought an old German army KDF jeep. Here were my first lessons in utility design. I can still remember all the details. Copies of *Vogue* magazine were borrowed from neighbours – the only indication that another world existed elsewhere. Evidence of creativity against the destruction going on around us.

1. Model aeroplanes. 2. Hop picking. 3. Marklin toy kit. 4. A. Ransome. 5. High-school building. 6. Holiday town of Trebon. 7. KDF car. 8. Concentration camp tower, 1952. 9. Czech radio. 10. Banknote.

155

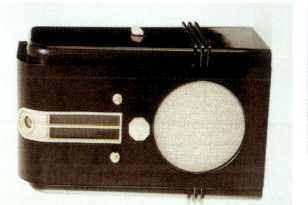

1951–1955

After battling hard to get into upper high school, life started to become more exciting. Why the battle? My father belonged to the bourgeoisie. Children of this class were not allowed to study at upper high school. School had become a total instrument of the regime propaganda. This was something to challenge. It was a different world elsewhere – the US, France, Britain. They had everything – food, jeans, chewing gum, books, magazines, and of course beautiful girls. I was just fifteen. The only real contact was via the radio. AFN (American Forces Network), later Radio Luxembourg. Jazz. Sinatra. Radio Free Europe, Voice of America for news. It was jammed, of course, but the only contact with outside world. There were no visual images. We could only guess what new things looked like. One could hear music, but only guess the faces. That hunger for visual information will stay with me for the rest of my life. My first drawings in preparation for architectural school exams were of course classical, and of course I was not accepted. Politically I was the wrong person, and I didn't know Czech grammar very well. I had to go to the State design office as a draughtsman. The cleaning of ruling pens was my main task. I was working in a modern building, but on projects in socialist–realism style. Collecting cigarette packets to help my friends visit their fathers in prison.

1. JK Drawing, 1953. 2. Socialist–realism architecture. 3. *Vogue* magazine. 4. Poster. 5. Food queue. 6. JK 'Dunkerque' model, 1953. 7. State design office. 8. JK 'Endeavour' model, 1952. 9. Tatra 603 car.

157

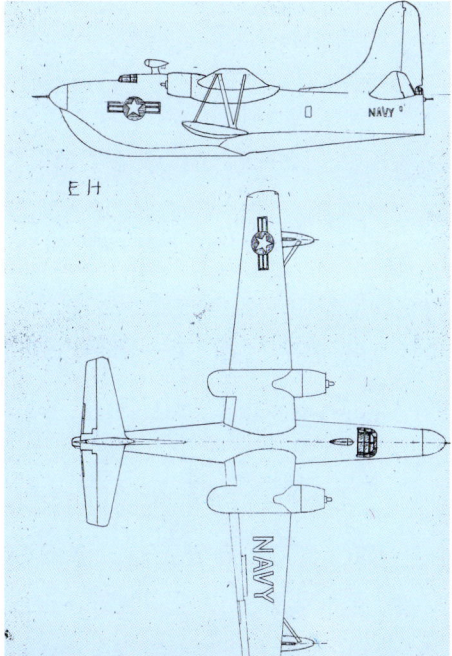

1955–1958

I was finally accepted at architecture school – the School of Applied Art and Architecture. I tried to look the other way. I received my first architectural book from my godfather in New York – Frank Lloyd Wright American Architecture. I still have it. Later came the discovery of FLW's Unison House. At school we were to measure the gothic portal and modern chair. My first independent design work was a piece of furniture. Then came my first house sketch. It was not very good. Panic over how to design. It was so difficult. Then came my first studio conversion, for friends. I was twenty. What excitement. Next a Banister Fletcher book. My father introduced me to Le Corbusier books. He had quite a few. What a discovery. *Life* magazine was smuggled in with pictures of the Hungarian uprising in 1956. This was a true turning point for communists in Europe. There was disappointment that the West did not help. In the meantime, more bottles of wine were opened, more parties organised. My first serious dates. More beautiful girls around. I dreamt of distant places, where so much was happening architecturally. It was totally impossible to go abroad. Embassy cars were the only real presence of modern design. I hoped this would not last forever.

1. Radio Luxembourg. 2. B. Fletcher. 3. Cadillac car. 4. Architectural book. 5. F. L. Wright house. 6. JK Drawing, 1957. 7. Applied Arts School, Prague. 8. Prague, 1958. 9. F. L. Wright. 10. F. Sinatra.

1. RADIO LUXEMBOURG 208/1440 KHz

2. A HISTORY OF ARCHITECTURE ON THE COMPARATIVE METHOD — Sir Banister Fletcher

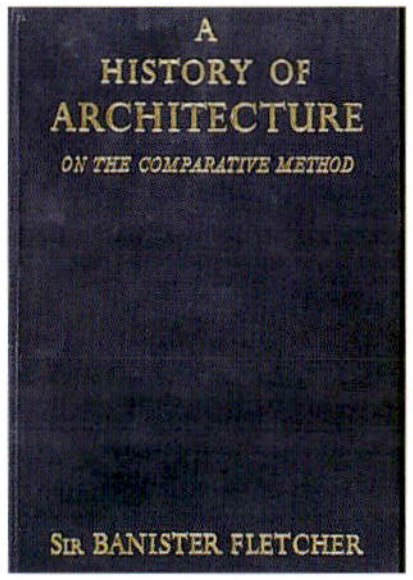

3.

4. BEFREITES WOHNEN

5.

6.

7.

8.

9. THE STORY OF THE TOWER — Frank Lloyd Wright

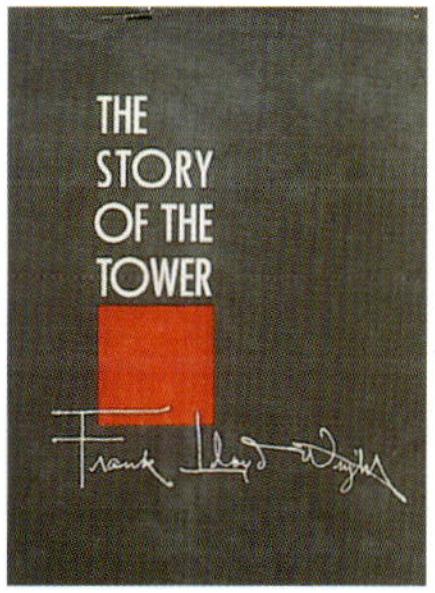

10.

159

1958–1960

Architectural school was going fine. I made further discoveries of important names. All by myself. There were few magazines. Few books. More architectural heroes. Absolutely no books in the bookshops. Fighting isolation. I was looking around for examples of Czech pre-war constructivist architecture. What did architects think in Europe, the US, South America? Libraries. I spent hours and hours at the University library. But these were hours of pleasure, inspiration, concentration and hope. Everything was a private discovery. Teachers said nothing, knew nothing. They were corrupted and sometimes scared of the regime. Yet they allowed you to do something modern. My parents bought a white Ford Anglia 1958 model. What excitement. In 1959 we took a trip to the USSR – the telephone books and town maps here were secret documents. But the American National Exhibition was there. Bucky's dome, Eames' furniture, Eames' seven-screen projection, Circorama. There were architectural books on shelves. I pinched one encouraged by exhibition staff. It was Le Corbusier's Modulor. I still have it. Then my first drink of Coca-cola. More hopes. Soviet horror all around.

1. Disability vehicle. 2. B. Bardot. 3. *Arts and Architecture* magazine. 4. JK Sketch, 1958. 5. JK Roof flat, 1958. 6. US Pavilion Exhibition, Moscow. 7. Le Corbusier. 8. JK Exhibition design, 1960.

161

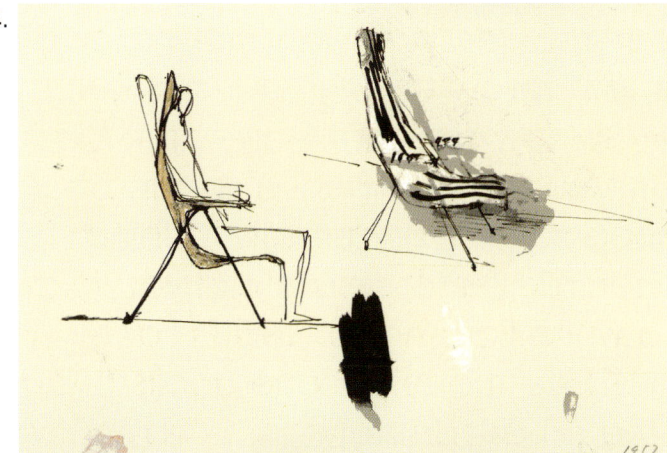

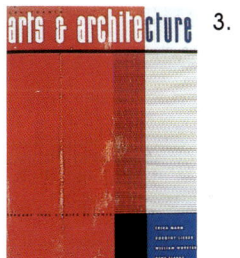

1960–1962

I took architecture very seriously. Not just architectural school. My first few private jobs. An ancient roof space in a flat. Artists' exhibition designs. My first house design. Of course this was not built. New influences. A K. Wachsman book, Bucky's exhibition catalogue. Endless discussions with fellow students. My first sketches for my diploma project. This was my choice – a new National Gallery in Prague. No drawings survive. Nights were spent working on the drawings. A space-deck model of the roof. Three thousand aluminium rod pieces. A kindergarten design two years before. Then a tragedy. My father died, partially out of sorrow. He never saw my diploma project. A part of my life was over. Then came Le Corbusier's book *My Work*. This was, and still is a major influence. Written by the man himself. It gives a very private and personal view. I was totally taken by this book. In a month's time I was drafted. Two years were wasted. I still tried to work on competitions at night. Reading Bucky's book on guard duty. But it was not possible. More hopes and dreams. One day…

1. Tu-104 aeroplane. 2. Film poster. 3. Le Corbusier. 4. JK House sketch, 1961. 5. JK Kindergarten, 1961. 6. R. D. Fuller catalogue. 7. Prague, 1962. 8. E. Presley. 9. Prague, 1962.

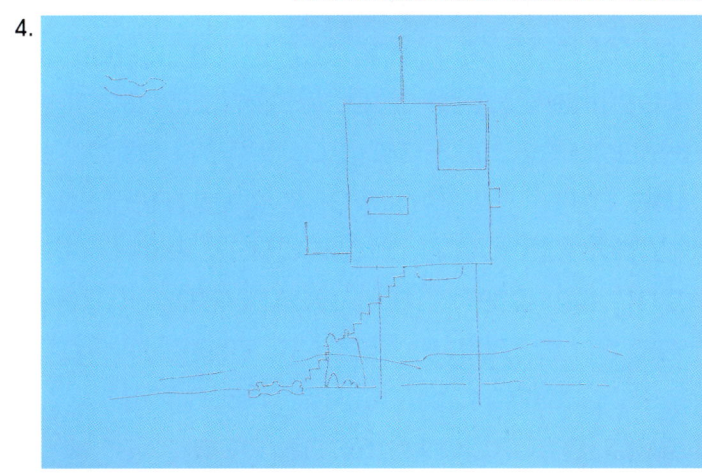

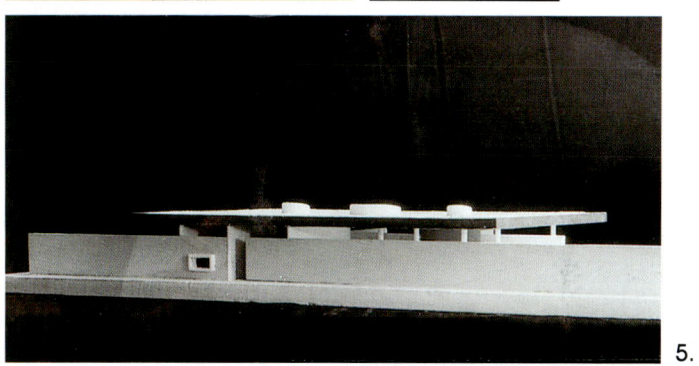

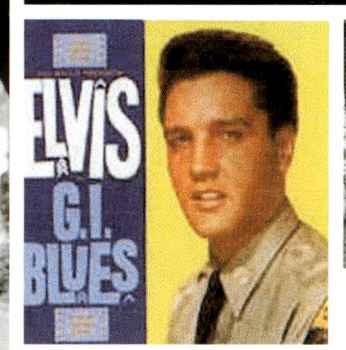

1.

2.

3.

4.

5.

6.

7.

8.

9.

163

1962–1964

Two years were wasted serving a hideous regime as an army private. What horror. Stupid people in command. Sometimes I could go home. I took part in a competition for a new town hall in Prague. Of course I was not successful. I was still going to the library, discovering new names like C. Ellwood, K. Wachsman. Reading *Arts and Architecture*. The case study houses programme was a nice discovery. Finally I was discharged from the army. I will never forget the feeling I had the next morning sitting behind the drawing board. Now what? No excuses. A few little jobs. You could not do real building privately. That was the law. Then a fantastic thing happened. I was able to go on a guided tour to the US. What an opportunity for me to see all those famous buildings. Suddenly architectural reality was here. My first flight ever – a 24-hour stop in London. I remember every detail. Huge posters on every corner. Colours. People. Then New York. The Seagram building. I had a private tour. Even a little picture on the wall played an important role. The Museum of Modern Art and its beautiful garden, and above all the *Architecture without Architects* book. What a shock. Seeing old beauty with modern eyes. I still have the book. Should I stay? I was not ready yet.

1. J. Cash LP. 2. *Architecture without Architects*. 3. A. Warhol. 4. *Domov* magazine. 5. JK Prague studio, 1967. 6. New York.
7. K. Honzik. 8. JK Town hall competition, 1964. 9. International driving licence. 10. Case study houses.

165

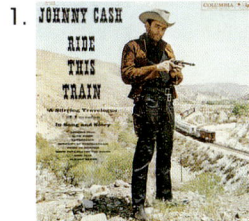

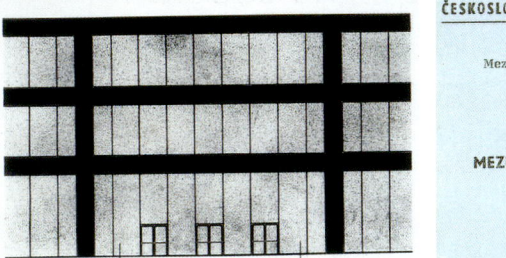

1964–1966

In New York I met my first real client. There were conversations about his new house. New garden. Mini-golf rails. Ramp connection. Furniture. I imported the first Eames chair to Prague. *Forum* magazine arrived with pictures of the Stirling Leicester building. Suddenly there was something different and new after Le Corbusier, Mies and others. Image created quite a lot of confusion and anxiety for me. Another strong influence was the *Case study houses* book I bought in the US. Here was another source of inspiration. Truly modern houses. Now second or even third generation after modern classics. Meanwhile, my time was spent sitting in the Slavia café and organising parties. Almost every day. Gallons of cheap wine were consumed. Plans were discussed. Beautiful girls were everywhere. Sometimes it was difficult to concentrate on architecture. The hideous regime was still very active all around. But people were less afraid to speak openly. I was still living in my parents house. There was no other option. I even established my office there. Three tables and one telephone line. My mother making coffee sometimes.

1. Letter. 2. Slavia café, Prague. 3. Twiggy. 4. *Playboy* magazine. 5. JK's Bedroom. 6. Y. Friedman. 7. P. Johnson. 8. J. Stirling. 9. Summer house. 10. JK Garden ramp, 1965

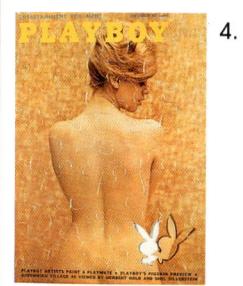

1.

2.

3.

4.

5.

6.

7.

8.

9.

10.

167

1966–1968

New influences, new thoughts. Yet my situation was not helped by the dictatorial regime around. One spent more time battling, cheating the regime, than doing new drawings. One day somebody sent me a copy of *Archigram* magazine. What a shock. Now truly everything was architecture. It certainly opened new gates. Suddenly there were new possibilities, more objects, more building types had become part of architectural thinking. This was particularly new in the part of Europe I was in at that time. But also new everywhere. My first house project was being built. I was learning new and bitter lessons. Simple, simple construction. It had to be. It was mostly built by the artist client himself. Then there was Prague Spring. We were quite sceptical. Communists allowing basic freedoms? That was almost a contradiction, it was unthinkable. You could buy copies of *Life* and *Time*, and books. The radio was not jammed. Travel became reasonably possible. it lasted only six months. On 21 August 1968 somebody woke me up by telephone at 3 o'clock, 'they are here, just listen'. He was right. Hundreds of tanks, total occupation. Russians. We truly hated them. In the first few hours our thoughts were how to get out. And I did. I could not go through it again, I wanted to do architecture and be free.

1. JK Film actor. 2. Magazine cover. 3. Le Corbusier. 4. JK Sketch 1967. 5. JK Photomontage, 1967. 6. JK F. Dvorak House, Prague, 1967. 7. Prague, 1968. 8. *Archigram* magazine. 9. Banknote.

169

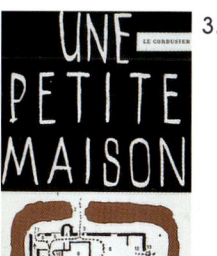

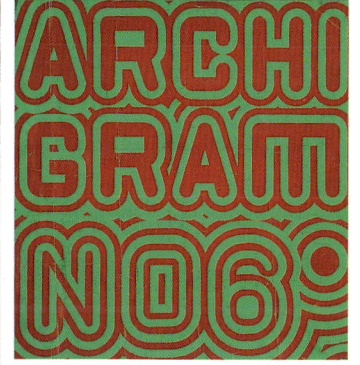

1968–1972

It was certainly a shock to arrive at Victoria Station in London, with practically nowhere to go and very little money. About $100 and two pairs of socks. Will they let me in? Austria certainly did. Switzerland did. They certainly did in England. There were 140,000 of us on the run. They issued us with Green Cards. That meant one could stay. People were kind. Government was kind. The next problem was to get a job. Where? How? Then began a series of miserable jobs. I was finally accepted in my first serious office – Denys Lasdun. I worked on drawings for the new National Theatre. Swinging London was still in full swing. Miniskirts and maxi coats were everywhere. What a pleasure to go and buy a book, magazine or even a newspaper. Subscriptions for *Life* and *Time* magazines. All this did not exist before. New inspirations. Discovering A. C. Clarke's *Profiles of the future*, Craig Ellwood's Monograph. Strong influences on my architectural thinking. The amazing excitement of man landing on the moon. That was something truly historical. What a technology, what a people. Eventually I got a job in an office I wanted to be in – Piano + Rogers. We were only six people altogether, before the Pompidou Centre competition was won. This was a totally unique and new office, even on the English architecture scene. Finally.

1. Summer session, 1970. 2. A. C. Clarke. 3. P*aris Match* magazine. 4. R. and S. Rogers. 5. Union Jack. 6. London, 1968. 7. C. Ellwood. 8. National Theatre, London. 9. *Newsweek* magazine. 10. JK Studio, London, 1972.

1.
2.
3.
4.
5.
6.
7.
8.
9.
10.

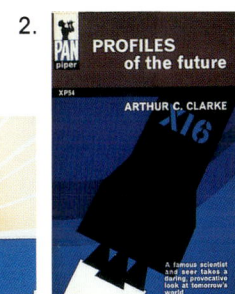

171

1972–1976

Being a job architect on a roof extension at Piano + Rogers was a hair-raising experience for me. I needed the help of a lot of people. Then came a fantastic victory for Piano + Rogers in Paris. Plateau Beaubourg. First out of 650 entries. We were an office of eight people, me sticking Letraset on one drawing. This was a historical moment. It will probably never happen again. The world was ready for new architectural talent. An extraordinary jury – J. Prouvé, O. Niemeyer, P. Johnson. Not a set of project managers. Fantastic. Then getting a new grey refugee passport. The possibility of travel for the first time, but very little money to do so. New influences. The Jean Prouvé discovery. Reading B. Fuller books. I went to see the film *2001* several times. It was magic, especially the abstract flat object that comes at the end. One could see the possibility of the arrival of a new world. Then change. I started at Foster Associates for the first time. I worked on the Willis Faber building – probably the first building ever exactly fitting an old urban pattern. A curvy building. The first use of a computer program. The critical decision to start to do my own drawings, projects. Every evening, every Saturday or Sunday. Desperately looking for my own expression. A telephone call from my mother every Sunday morning. The communist regime in Prague was getting more and more aggressive. More people were being destroyed there.

1. J. Prouvé. 2. JK Cabin 380, 1975. 3. *2001* film. 4. Architectural design. 5. Summer house, Switzerland. 6. JK Photomontage, 1972. 7. Piano + Rogers Roof extension, London, 1972. 8. St. Tropez, 1973. 9. Letter.

1.
2.
3.
4.
5.
6.
7.
8.
9.

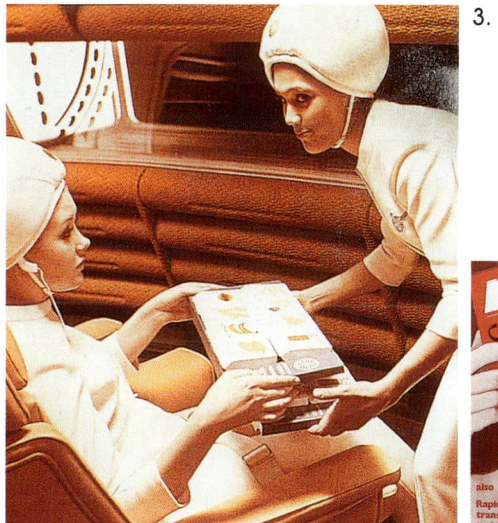

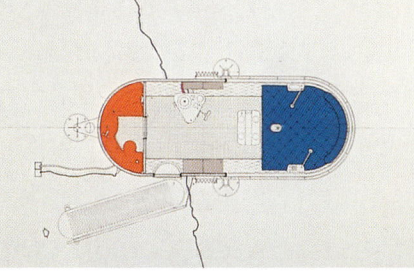

173

1976–1979

Finally, in 1976 came my UK citizenship and passport. A visit to US. A visit to Eames' house in Los Angeles. Tea with Ray Eames will stick in my mind forever. All this was rapidly changing my vision of the architectural world. My work on Brighton Marina. The unusual design possibilities suppressed by those around me like many times before. Then my first actual built design, conversion of a flat at Archery Steps in London. New thinking, particularly in furniture. New materials. A flight on Concorde. Mach 2 – twice the speed of sound. The world was changing. Then in 1976, David Nixon and I entered a small competition for an industrial unit. We were awarded one of the three first prizes. This was quite an achievement for both of us. Working with structural engineer T. Hunt at Hanscomb as quantity surveyor, we thought we could make it. Of course the other two schemes were built, but not ours. It was too radical, not just different. This was the first achievement of Future Systems, without the name. The prospect of starting our own office had become real. But of course this happened only much, much later. I started to wonder whether I would ever break through. Nobody believed in my knowledge of architecture or practical experience. In 1977 I started at Foster Associates for the second time. I was 40.

1. C. and R. Eames. 2. R. B. Fuller. 3. Concorde information. 4. UK passport. 5. JK Archery Steps flat, London, 1974. 6. FS factory, 1976. 7. Beetle car. 8. Brighton Marina. 9. Art-Net Gallery. 10. American Express card.

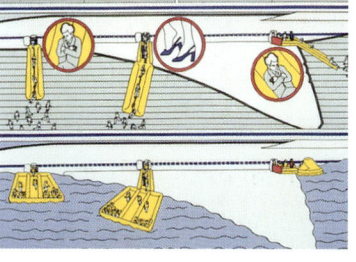

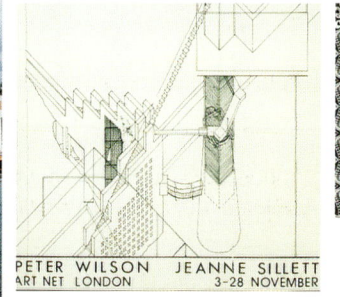

1.

2.

3.

4.

5.

6.

7.

8.

9.

10.

175

1979–1982

I was still working at Foster Associates in 1979. I had a strong feeling that something very different would happen. It was quite an exciting time there. Hong Kong Shanghai Bank particularly. The Humana Project and many others. Much of it was innovative and exciting. But David Nixon and I felt strongly that we should start our own office. We were in touch daily. One day in 1979, sitting in the car, we came up with the name. Future Systems. On registering the name we were amazed that nobody else was called the same. Great. We had the name, but the company had absolutely no work. We had to keep working for others. Me in Foster's and David in Grimshaw's. We even had a business card. Then came the first real job, a flat conversion for Deyan Sudjic, editor of *Blueprint*. This was quite an innovative solution for a classic problem. A Victorian building. We inserted aluminium platforms for new functions. Many people liked it. Magazines liked it. The oval aluminium opening became almost a symbol of the practice. My private life was also in turmoil. Every Saturday was spent working on private projects. More and more exciting ones. I built more model aeroplanes.

1. FS Deyan Sudjic flat, London, 1983. 2. RIBA *Journal*. 3. Le Corbusier. 4. FS Business card. 5. A. Frey. 6. JK 45° house, 1981. 7. Nice, France. 8. NASA report. 9. Model aeroplane.

1.
2.
3.
4.
5.
6.
7.
8.
9.

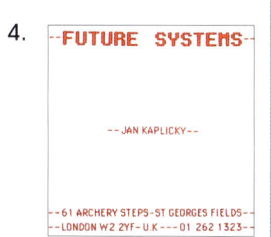

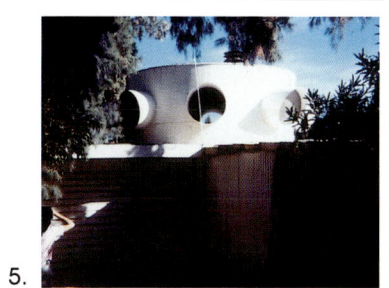

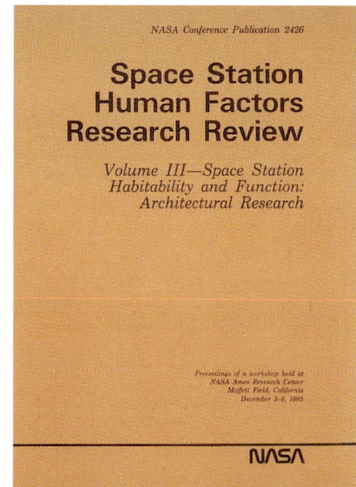

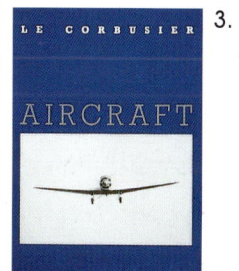

177

1982–1986

In 1983 I was fired from Foster Associates. This of course created a new situation. Suddenly Future Systems became a full-time job. It happened one Friday. So-called black Friday. I was already teaching at the Architectural Association, but this could not provide the resources for even minimal living. But soon came our first jobs. Eva Jiricna and Future Systems designed the Way-In floor for Harrods in London. It was quite fascinating to design a whole new image. Even a new logo and shopping bag. Production capacity was minimal. Sitting alone in a tiny studio with one telephone line did not help. Then a certain chapter in my life closed forever. My mother died. I will never forget that day. It is certainly an unbelievable shock when your mother dies. The last link to your childhood is suddenly gone. Forever. However some positive things were to come. We were invited to take part in an exhibition in Paris – 'Nouvelles Tendances'. Future Systems had several projects there including the NASA table mock-up, and the Doughnut house mock-up made in a boatyard. Our old dreams were coming true. Our knowledge of boat production had come to use ten years on. Future Systems in action. Future Systems was now on the architecture map. Just.

1. Banknote. 2. FS Doughnut house, 1985. 3. NASA Spin-off book. 4. FS Way-In shop, Harrods, 1984. 5. FS AA Exhibition, London, 1987. 6. FS Architectural Association Book, 1987. 7. *Architecture d'Aujourdhui*. 8. Architects Journal. 9. Letter.

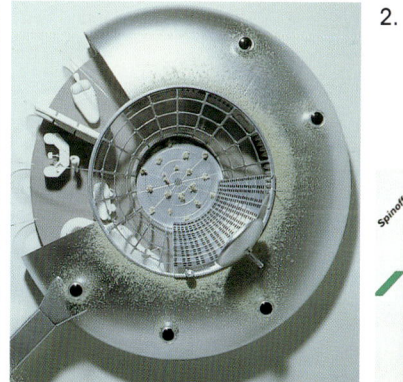

1.
2.
3.
4.
5.
6. FUTURE SYSTEMS
7.
8.
9.

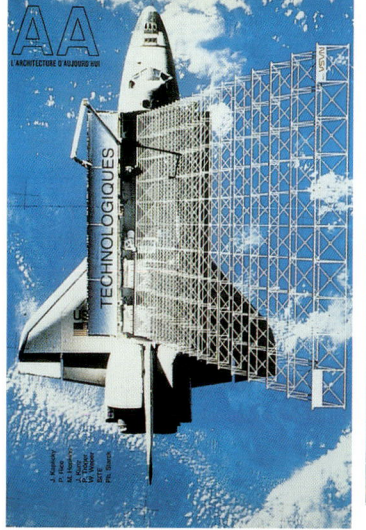

179

1986–1989

David Nixon had already been to California. This had generated a lot of interest in space projects, several of which materialised on several levels. A totally new world. But one felt a certain need for change in architecture. New expression, new form. Use of eco systems. Use of daylight. A spin-off from the technical innovations used in space projects. The opportunity presented itself in a competition for Grand buildings on Trafalgar Square in London. The result was certainly revolutionary – even for Future Systems. Maybe in architecture generally. It clearly signalled new thinking and form. When shown in lectures as much as ten years later people would laugh. Not any more. There is dead silence. It was 1986. Fifteen years later people began to copy it – a clear indication of the extremely slow evolution in architecture. I went to Ronchamp chapel for the first time after all those years. The sloping floor was a complete surprise. The astonishing beauty of the whole object. A true masterpiece. One felt that the last days of communism were on the horizon. Finally, on 17 November 1989, came the Velvet revolution in Prague. Technology destroyed communism. It was the computer revolution. Satellite television. The Xerox machine. Suddenly there were millions of free people in Europe. Before this, in 1987, I met Amanda Levete. My new life began.

1. Salt and pepper. 2. F. Kiesler. 3. 'Nouvelles Tendances' Exhibition, Paris. 4. Czech functionalism. 5. FS Blob, London, 1985. 6. Prague, 1989. 7. China, 1989. 8. JK and Ronchamp chapel. 9. Prague, 1990.

1.
2.
3.
4.
5.
6.
7.
8.
9.

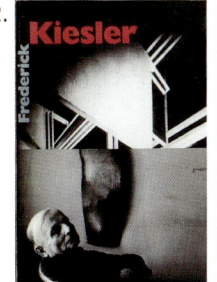

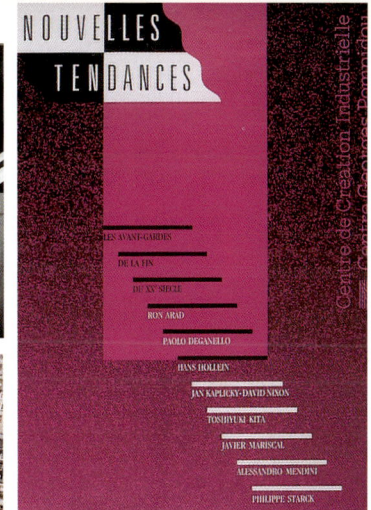

181

1989–1993

Next came another fantastic opportunity. Future Systems was selected with nineteen others to take part in a competition for the Bibliotheque Nationale in Paris. What a task. At the time we were only three people. This was a big building – 200,000 square metres of building on an interesting site on the river with a possible bridge connection. Future Systems was by now in new office space. That space could accommodate fifteen people – total luxury. Finally it became an independent office. Our design for the Bibliotheque was quite radical. It indicated a very sculptural object. Plasticity – very new in those days. It was amazing to see the other projects. Sometimes they were one or two generations behind. We got second prize. What an achievement. President Mitterand of course chose a more conventional project. This was a great disappointment but also a sense of victory. The extraordinary feeling of what just three people can do. The project still looks unique after all these years. I had stopped teaching at the Architectural Association. I am not a born teacher. And almost immediately after the Bibliotheque we started work on another competition for a New Museum of the Acropolis. Here we lost in the first round, rejected by people who it seems don't know anything about architecture. But it is still one of our best projects. Admired by many. It was 1989.

1. Caprice restaurant, London. 2. Y. Klein. 3. FS book, 1993. 4. FS Bibliotheque National, Paris, 1989. 5. FS Office, London, 1989. 6. B. Clarke. 7. Stamp. 8. Fashion, 1989. 9. Storefront gallery, New York.

183

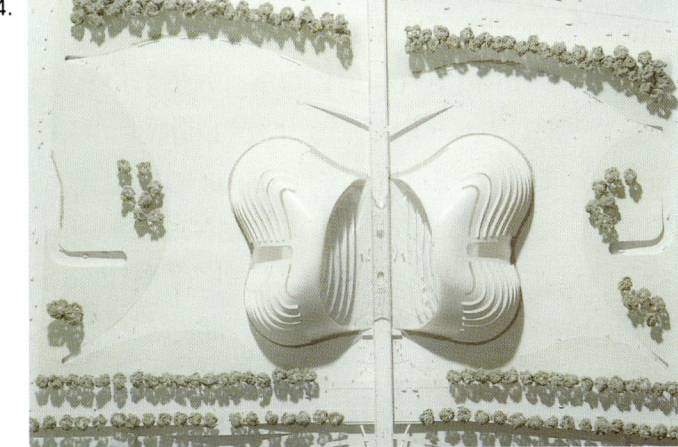

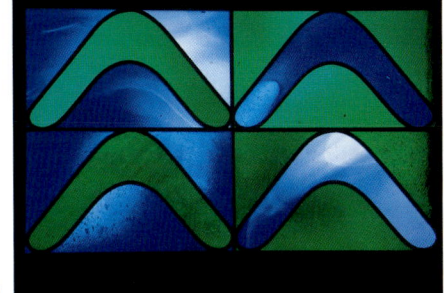

1993–1996

The first book on Future Systems was published. I remember those hours and hours spent designing every page – 156 of them. The book put us firmly on the map. Even internationally. It sold more than 12,000 copies. Another book – *For Inspiration Only* – was at the design stage. My long-time dream was finally published. It had been rejected by five different publishers. We started the design of the house in Islington. This was a very difficult site. To accommodate more than 200 square metres was almost impossible. The house was completed and became more commonly known as the Glass House. Even London taxi drivers know where it is. In a country where so few modern houses are built, the house became a symbol of modern residential architecture. We had here an extraordinary client. This was an essential part of the story. A special book was published on the house. I then visited the Tropics for the first time. Harbour Island in the Bahamas with its pink sand and clear blue water was certainly an amazing inspiration. How would one design a house there? The climate here suddenly introduces different challenges. In 1995 my son Josef was born on my birthday. What a 'present'. We moved to a new flat and converted the garage. Finally we had some living space around us.

'We are projected to have a hundred million AIDS cases by 2005.' B. Clinton

1. Harbour Island, Bahamas. 2. FS Hauer/King house book. 3. JK *For Inspiration Only* book. 4. FS House in Wales, 1984. 5. FS Hillgate Street flat, London, 1996. 6. J. Kolar. 7. Josef Kaplicky Jnr. 8. Red ball. 9. O. Niemeyer.

1.

2.

3.

4.

5.

6.

7.

8.

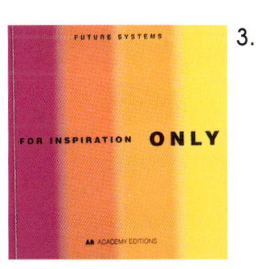

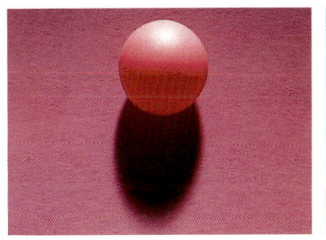

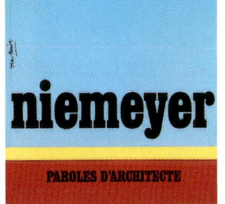

9.

185

1996–2001

This was an exciting time. In 1995 we won the competition to design the Media Centre at Lord's Cricket Ground. It was a quite revolutionary design. An aluminium semi-monocoque structure built in a boatyard. All fire-proofed. Not many people would have dared to suggest this. It was finally completed in 1999. A great success with cricket writers, TV and radio. A nice place to have a drink. There was not a single negative comment from its users. 'We love it Jan', they told me. The press called it all sorts of names. But these people only write about architecture. They are not designers and builders. Future Systems also had a few very successful exhibitions. At the ICA in London, 30,000 people came. There were queues outside. We had the same success in Prague. Thousands of young people came – very young. But there was not a single commission. After the Media Centre we had no work at all. Our financial resources were down to zero. Being awarded the Stirling Prize helped. Then suddenly Selfridges came along and commissioned us to design a 25,000 square metres department store in Birmingham. Just like that. What a vision, what trust. Future Systems was safe. A new chapter began.

**'Germany builds as many wind farms in a week as Britain does in a year.'
The Independent, 2001**

1. Stirling Prize party. 2. Balkans War. 3. FS Catalogue, 1999. 4. FS ICA Exhibition, London, 1996. 5. FS Lord's Media Centre, London, 1994. 6. Josef Kaplicky Jnr. Bridge. 7. Stirling Prize. 8. Brasserie Lipp, Paris.

1.

2.

3.

4.

5.

6.

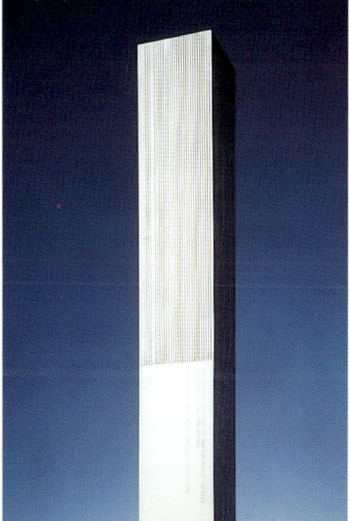

7.

8.

187

TODAY

What is happening today? Future Systems is operating from a large office in the middle of London, and building in several countries. The comfort of a big space is remarkable. The luxury of a proper library. A display of our previous work. Hundreds of models around. Space for several meetings. Even the coffee tastes better. More jobs, more struggles. Every day there are new victories, new battles. Everyday one is asking questions. Is anybody interested in architecture? Does anybody care about better buildings? Design? Architecture? Environment? Pollution? Beauty? Comfort? The people using the buildings? I am afraid that very few do seem to care. The armada of people associated with every project certainly do not. Even many clients do not. We are getting more and more involved in various special interiors. Mostly fashion shops. It is fascinating what can be achieved with the transformation of a very ordinary space. Knowledge of materials is essential. Knowledge of manufacturing techniques is important. People who can physically make things are vital. Producing just drawing after drawing is not enough. The process of creating new reality is rewarding. It is a private process. It certainly does not take place in meetings.

'Today fiber-optic cable can transmit 30 million calls across the Atlantic a second.' *Time* magazine

1. Stamp. 2. Chrysler car. 3. Pokemon card. 4. I. Margolius. 5. FS Marni shop, London, 2000. 6. FS Office, London, 2000. 7. Today's people. 8. Marni fashion. 9. FS *Unique Building*, 2001. 10. Banknote.

189

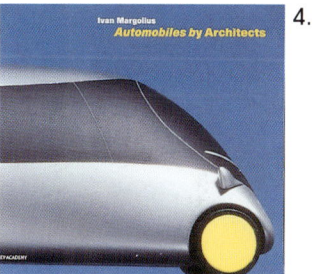

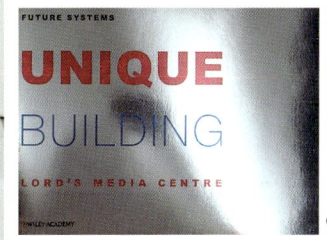

TODAY

In the meantime, life goes on. Architectural problems are a tiny fraction of people's lives. The Selfridges department store is finally onsite and is being built. It is moving ahead fast. From a big, big hole to the finished building in 2003. Finally one can use all that knowledge collected over 40 years. All that knowledge people deny. Introducing elements and techniques on the Selfridges job, never used before. It is a pleasure and a challenge to have a client who understands modern architecture. Vittorio Radice. Who not only understands architecture and design but of course understands modern shopping. We discuss principles, not types of door handles. How very rare. The battle for modern architecture continues in Britain. Sadly it is still considered a foreign import by many. The gap between architects onsite, developers and the construction industry is widening. The design and build system is taking over whole continents – Asia and North America. Will Europe survive its unique and progressive architectural role? I do not know. I hope so.

'One quarter of the people on the earth never get a clean glass of water.'
B. Clinton

1. Airline sugar. 2. R. Rogers. 3. High Society, 2001. 4. Invitation. 5. FS BMW Munich, 2001. 6. FS Villa Noci, Italy, 2001. 7. New in old. 8. Pollution. 9. Parking. 10. A. Camus.

1.
2.
3.
4.
5.
6.
7.
8.
9.
10.

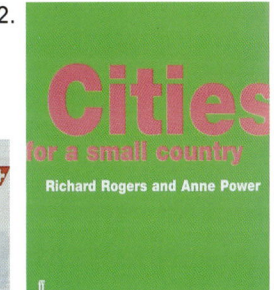

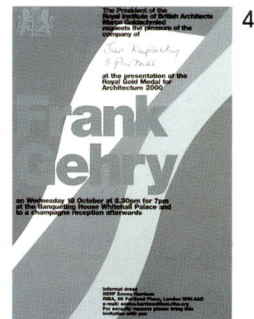

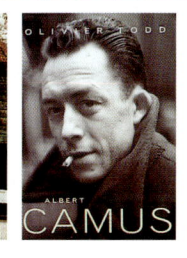

191

TODAY

Latest projects such as the Ferrari stands, Galliano shop, Selfridges building or even the Alessi coffee and tea set reflecting the latest thinking, knowledge and skill. But are they progressive enough? Is one going far enough? Do they initiate the future of their category? Will they still be valuable in the next few years? Can one still be called architectural avant-garde? All projects require a philosophy. A purpose. Do others share these thoughts? One is learning from and admiring the organisation of skills and purpose of big engineering or space projects. Almost always the results are more clear, progressive and even beautiful. Phenomenal progress in the design of cameras, computers, aeroplanes and cars must be considered a challenge for architects and the building industry. There is a need for research projects. They can be true avant-garde. The same as racing cars for the car industry. They are particularly vital in architecture. Future Systems has carried out quite a few research projects. Testing-ground for new forms and engineering. Green systems. It is unusual for the government to support architectural projects. But we have one. The advanced school unit.

'I want to drag British architects out in the street and shoot them.'
B. Sheeman, Labour MP, 2002.

1. New camera. 2. New York, 11 September 2001. 3. Scooter. 4. *Architecture Today* magazine. 5. *Architectural Design* magazine. 6. FS MAB restaurant, Amsterdam, 2001. 7. Demonstration. 8. Africa, 2001. 9. European Union. 10. Stamp.

1.

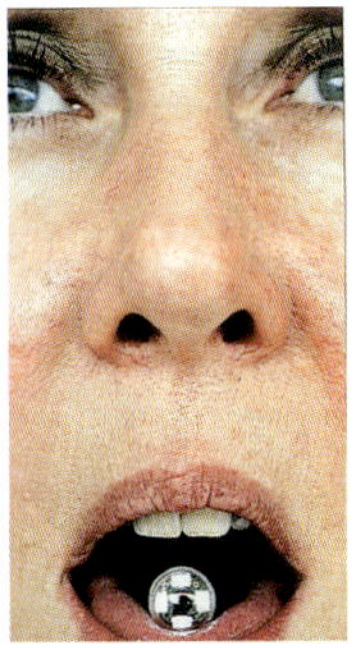

2.

3.

4. ARCHITECTURE TODAY · 94

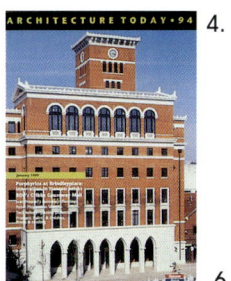

5. Looking Back in Envy

6.

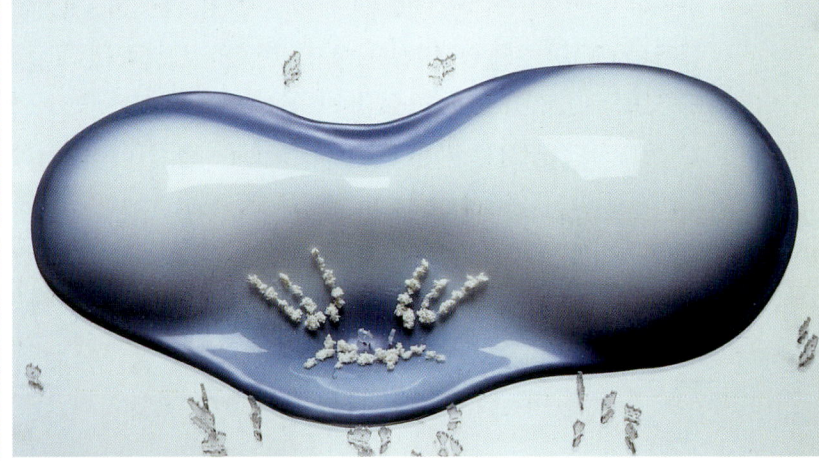

7.

8.

9.

10. 1ST

193

FUTURE

Looking ahead only 15 or 20 years. What will change? What will not? Will anything change at all? According to some developers and writers, architecture will no longer exist. This is nonsense. Maybe it will have a new name, a new image, new materials and new colours. Perhaps new meaning. Have we achieved anything at all as the modern movement? Yes, quite a lot. But look at the films predicting this period. We are not there yet. Maybe we shall never be. Brave thinking and forward thinking are required. Vision. Some critical projects will be still sitting on the drawing board or screen in a hundred years. Maybe there will be some progress in exploration of the universe. Certainly a station on Mars is planned. Certainly colonisation, mining and exploration of the Moon. Solar energy beamed from outer space – a critical new source of energy that might even change the political situation globally. Oil will lose its political power. There will be free solar or wave power. It is about time. Discovery of forms of life on another planet? Maybe.

'UK Government has vowed to produce 20% of electricity needs from renewable energy by 2010'. The Guardian, 2001

1. Chemical warfare 2. Architecture. 3. Government book. 4. *Metropolis* film, 1926. 5. Stamp. 6. South America. 7. Energy from space. 8. New vision. 9 NASA space station.

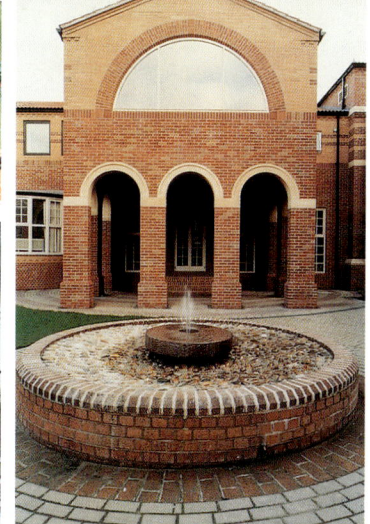

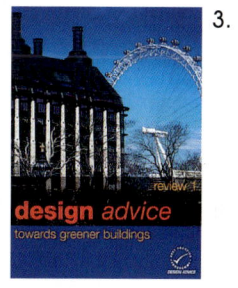

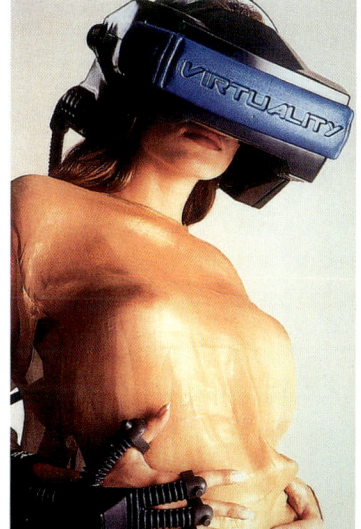

1.

2.

4.

5.

3.

7.

8.

6.

9.

195

FUTURE

Of course more horrible, useless buildings will be constructed. Buildings not designed to help people live or enjoy life. Buildings to satisfy only financial arrangements. Buildings not built by architects. Buildings with no relationship to life. Hopefully a new generation of beautiful, sophisticated, easy-to-live-in buildings will come. Even more beautiful. Charming. Plastic. Elegant. Efficient. Colourful. Sensual. Sexual. They will not just be commercial products, but products of love, care, knowledge and skill. Products of sophisticated production methods already used in the car and aircraft industries. Probably no 'new' materials, or perhaps only a very few. New production methods not just on the drawing board. Of course all will be eco buildings, prefabricated buildings. But they will not be designed to last hundreds of years, instead maybe only twenty-five or so. The basic structure for longer. Lots of green spaces inside and out for the people. They will have to relate to modern urban and transport requirements. Back to beauty. Back to people. Of course. Naturally.

'Factory manufactured housing will be the norm by 2020.' BT Laboratories

1. Detroit town centre. 2. Monarchy. 3. Mass production. 4. Banknote. 5. Printed circuit. 6. Architecture. 7. Contrast. 8. Levitation train. 9. Contraceptive patch.

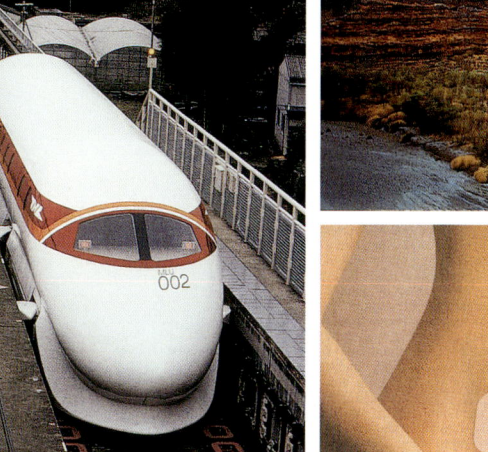

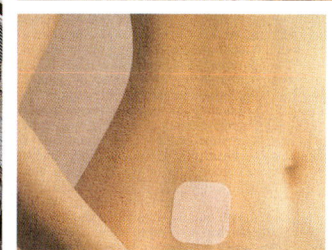

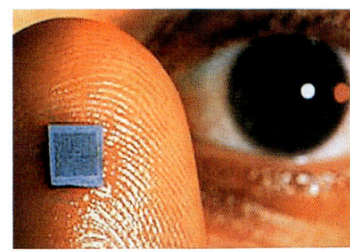

1.

2.

3.

4.

5.

6.

7.

8.

9.

FUTURE

Will people change? Radically? Certainly not. Will they look different? Probably not. Will they dress differently? Certainly yes. Will they still read books and magazines? Just. Will art galleries and libraries still exist? Yes. People will use hundreds of gadgets and mechanisms to support their life. Will they love good food? Will they eat less junk food? Probably. Will they make love? Certainly. Will they have dates? Probably not. Only onscreen conversations. New urban and transport patterns must be implemented, particularly public transport systems. The magic electric bus. The electric car. The vast urban decline especially in the US must be stopped. Otherwise radical political solutions will quickly appear. Decisions may be made on the streets, not in parliament. The evergrowing population on the planet needs houses, buildings, transport. First of all homes. But these cannot be built with a few bricks and mortar, as in Roman times. Another industrial architectural revolution? Probably yes. It is almost impossible to predict the future. How fundamentally wrong one can be. But above all, love and beauty will survive. And certainly many of us will no longer be here.

'A world population greater than 7.5 billion by 2020.' BT Laboratories

1. Station on Mars. 2. Future food. 3. Boeing Sonic cruiser. 4. Crises. 5. Architecture. 6. N. Tchernikov, 1922. 7. Future fashion. 8. Artificial heart.

1.
2.
3.
4.
5.
6.
7.
8.

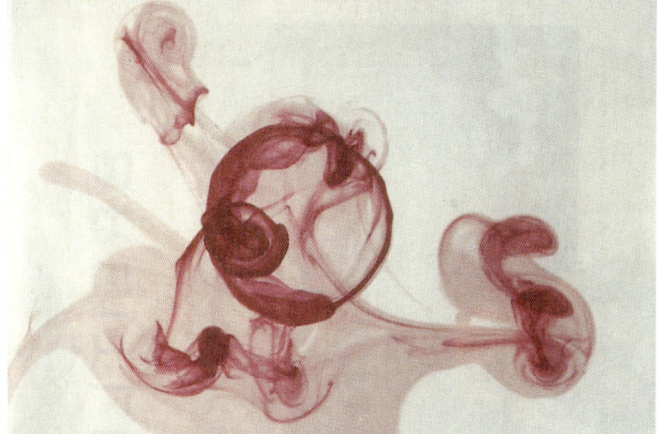

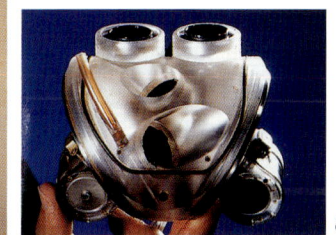

199

LAST WORD

I do not have a large black hat or glasses with a blue rim. I am not gay, Jewish, English or rich. Heaven forbid only Slav. From a country 'we know nothing about'. From peasant and distant 'Eastern' Europe. All this did not help. I am not even allowed to be called an architect. But I am. With forty years of battling for things more beautiful behind me. Still an incurable romantic. I still love women. I still love wine, brandy and chanterelles with caraway seeds. I would like to have one more friendship. One more intimate dinner in Paris. I can see a few things others cannot. They used to laugh at my projects, now they copy them. Maybe I will be allowed to build one museum, one house on the sea and one garden. I can see it now. Full of spirit, beauty, plasticity and colours. It is almost all finished. This book is a simple record of my thoughts, work and life. One day maybe…

'Architecture is an act of love, not a stage set.' Le Corbusier

1. Japanese maple tree planted 18/04/37, Prague.

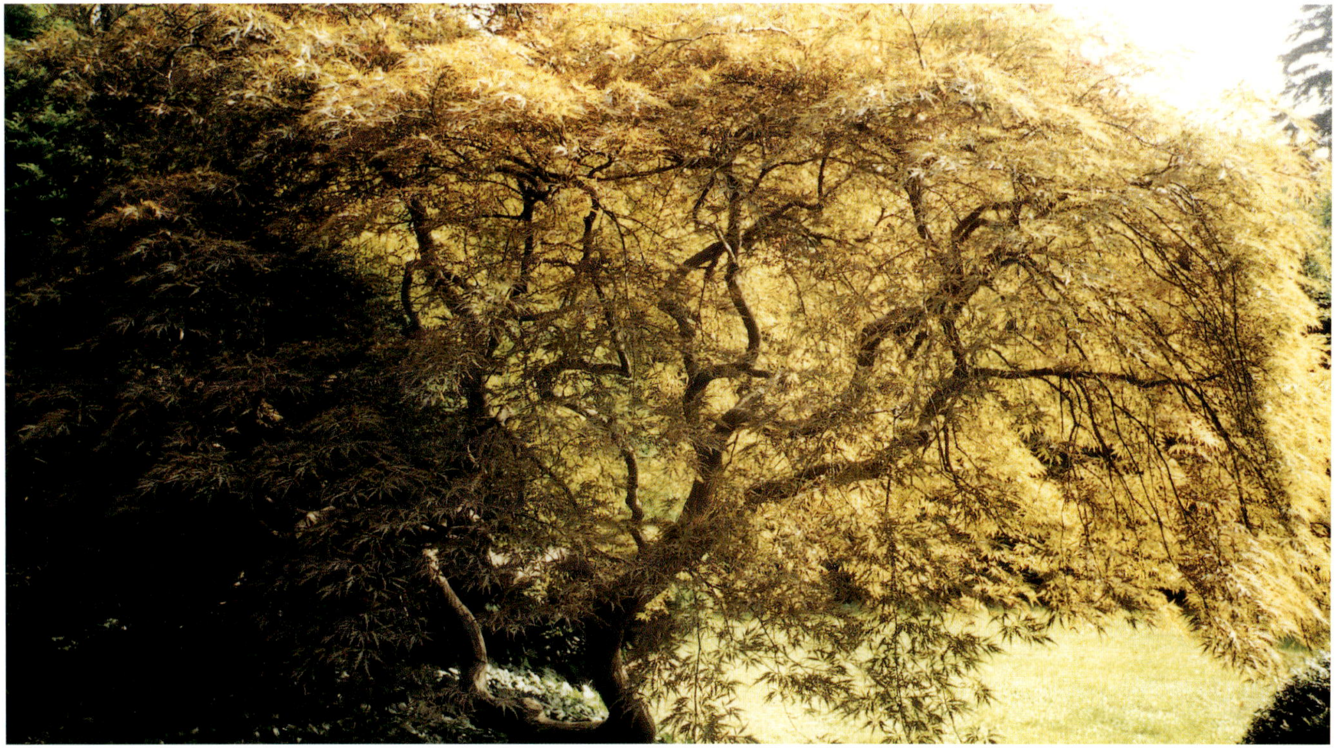

1937

202

2002

JAN KAPLICKY

1937	Born Prague, Czechoslovakia
1955-56	Draftsman in State design office
1956-62	College of Applied Art and Architecture
1962-64	National Service
1964-68	Private practice, Prague
1968	Arrival in Great Britain
1975	British citizenship
1979	Future Systems established with David Nixon
1982-86	Teaching at Architectural Association
1989	A. Levete joins Future Systems as partner
1995	Son Josef is born
1999	RIBA Stirling Prize
2000	Honorable Fellow RIBA

Gratitude and thanks

Rosy Head for transferring scribbles into a serious text in English. Dick Ernest, Milan Hromadka and Radka Cigler for providing unique material. Richard Davies for the beautiful photographs of Future Systems projects. Richard Learoyd for photographs of the Future Systems team. Don Shuttleworth for constructing the most beautiful models. And Maggie Toy, Mariangela Palazzi-Williams and Caroline Ellerby for changing a pile of material into a real book.

Every effort has been made to locate sources and credit materials but in any cases where this has not been possible our apologies are extended.

Published in Great Britain in 2002 by Wiley-Academy, a division of John Wiley & Sons Ltd

Copyright © 2002 - John Wiley & Sons Ltd, The Atrium, Southern Gate, Chichester, West Sussex PO19 8SQ, England
Telephone (+44) 1243 779777

Email (for orders and customer service enquiries): cs-books@wiley.co.uk
Visit our Home Page on www.wileyeurope.com or www.wiley.com

All Rights Reserved. No part of this publication may be reproduced, stored in a retrieval system or transmitted in any form or by any means, electronic, mechanical, photocopying, recording, scanning or otherwise, except under the terms of the Copyright, Designs and Patents Act 1988 or under the terms of a licence issued by the Copyright Licensing Agency Ltd, 90 Tottenham Court Road, London W1T 4LP, UK, without the permission in writing of the Publisher. Requests to the Publisher should be addressed to the Permissions Department, John Wiley & Sons Ltd, The Atrium, Southern Gate, Chichester, West Sussex PO19 8SQ, England, or emailed to permreq@wiley.co.uk, or faxed to (+44) 1243 770571.

ISBN 0-471-49541-7

Design and cover by Jan Kaplicky
Printed and bound in Italy
This book is printed on acid-free paper